First World War
and Army of Occupation
War Diary
France, Belgium and Germany

40 DIVISION
120 Infantry Brigade
Highland Light Infantry
14th (Service) Battalion
3 June 1916 - 30 April 1919

WO95/2612/1

The Naval & Military Press Ltd
www.nmarchive.com
Published in association with The National Archives

Published by

The Naval & Military Press Ltd

Unit 10 Ridgewood Industrial Park,

Uckfield, East Sussex,

TN22 5QE England

Tel: +44 (0) 1825 749494

www.naval-military-press.com

www.nmarchive.com

This diary has been reprinted in facsimile from the original. Any imperfections are inevitably reproduced and the quality may fall short of modern type and cartographic standards.

© **Crown Copyright**
Images reproduced by permission of The National Archives, London, England, 2015.

Contents

Document type	Place/Title	Date From	Date To
Heading	WO95/2612 (1)		
Heading	40th Division 120th Infy Bde 14th Bn High'd Lt Infy. June 1916 1919 Apl.		
Heading	War Diary of the 14th (S) Bn Highland Light Infantry. From 3rd June 1916 to 30th June 1916 Vol 1		
War Diary	Blackdown	03/06/1916	03/06/1916
War Diary	Havre	04/06/1916	05/06/1916
War Diary	Lillers	06/06/1916	06/06/1916
War Diary	Ecquedecques	11/06/1916	11/06/1916
War Diary	Bethune	12/06/1916	12/06/1916
War Diary	In The Trenches	12/06/1916	16/06/1916
War Diary	Annequin	16/06/1916	23/06/1916
War Diary	Trenches.	21/06/1916	21/06/1916
War Diary	Annequin	23/06/1916	23/06/1916
War Diary	Annequin	24/06/1916	24/06/1916
War Diary	Bruay	25/06/1916	30/06/1916
Heading	War Diary of 14 (S) Highland Light Infantry 40 July 14 H L I Vol 2 Volume 2 (July 1916)		
War Diary	Bruay	01/07/1916	04/07/1916
War Diary	Les Brebis	11/07/1916	11/07/1916
War Diary	North Maroc	14/07/1916	15/07/1916
War Diary	In The Trenches	16/07/1916	16/07/1916
War Diary	Les Brebis	17/07/1916	22/07/1916
War Diary	Calonne	22/07/1916	27/07/1916
War Diary	Calonne	30/07/1916	30/07/1916
Heading	War Diary 14th (S) Bn Highland Light Infantry August 1916 Volume 3		
War Diary	Bully Crenay	01/08/1916	03/08/1916
War Diary	Loos	04/08/1916	09/08/1916
War Diary	Maroc	10/08/1916	12/08/1916
War Diary	Les Brebis	12/08/1916	16/08/1916
War Diary	Calonne	16/08/1916	23/08/1916
War Diary	Calonne	22/08/1916	22/08/1916
War Diary	Bully Grenay	24/08/1916	25/08/1916
War Diary	Les Brebis	30/08/1916	05/09/1916
War Diary	Maroc	05/09/1916	19/09/1916
War Diary	Petit Sains	19/09/1916	21/09/1916
War Diary	Loos 14 Bis	22/09/1916	22/09/1916
War Diary	Mazingarbe	26/09/1916	28/09/1916
War Diary	14 Bis	30/09/1916	30/09/1916
Heading	14th Highland Light Infantry Volume 5		
War Diary	Right Subsec 14. Bis	03/10/1916	03/10/1916
War Diary	Village Line 14 Bis.	04/10/1916	07/10/1916
War Diary	Right. Subsect. 14 Bis	08/10/1916	10/10/1916
War Diary	Philosophe	12/10/1916	17/10/1916
War Diary	Right. Subsection Hulluch	18/10/1916	24/10/1916
War Diary	Les Brebis	25/10/1916	25/10/1916
War Diary	Les Brebis	22/10/1916	22/10/1916
War Diary	Bruay	27/10/1916	27/10/1916
War Diary	La Thieuloye	28/10/1916	28/10/1916

War Diary	Bailleul And Cornailles	29/10/1916	01/11/1916
War Diary	Canettmont	02/11/1916	03/11/1916
War Diary	Villers L'Hopital	04/11/1916	04/11/1916
War Diary	Bernaville	05/11/1916	11/11/1916
War Diary	Doullens	12/11/1916	12/11/1916
War Diary	Souastre	13/11/1916	14/11/1916
War Diary	Hebuterne	15/11/1916	19/11/1916
War Diary	Coigneux	20/11/1916	21/11/1916
War Diary	Amplier	22/11/1916	22/11/1916
War Diary	Fieffes	23/11/1916	23/11/1916
War Diary	Gorenflos	24/11/1916	13/12/1916
War Diary	Stetoile	14/12/1916	14/12/1916
War Diary	Camp 13	15/12/1916	23/12/1916
War Diary	Camp III.	24/12/1916	25/12/1916
War Diary	Camp III Bouchavesnes North	26/12/1916	28/12/1916
War Diary	North Bouchavesnes	29/12/1916	30/12/1916
War Diary	Asquith Flats.	31/12/1916	31/12/1916
War Diary	Camp 17	31/12/1916	31/12/1916
War Diary	Camp 17 Suzanne Sur Somme	01/01/1917	04/01/1917
War Diary	Maurepas Ravine	04/01/1917	07/01/1917
War Diary	Maurepas Ravine	08/01/1917	08/01/1917
War Diary	Rancourt	09/01/1917	12/01/1917
War Diary	Camp. 17.	12/01/1917	18/01/1917
War Diary	Asquith Flats	19/01/1917	22/01/1917
War Diary	North Bouchavesnes	23/01/1917	26/01/1917
War Diary	Camp 124	26/01/1917	27/01/1917
War Diary	Corbie	27/01/1917	11/02/1917
War Diary	Camp 112	17/02/1917	27/02/1917
War Diary	Camp 112	12/02/1917	28/02/1917
War Diary	Camp 112 Bray.	01/03/1917	06/03/1917
War Diary	Camp 19	07/03/1917	07/03/1917
War Diary	Howitzer Wood	08/03/1917	09/03/1917
War Diary	Bethune Road	10/03/1917	17/03/1917
War Diary	Old. German Front. Line	18/03/1917	18/03/1917
War Diary	Support. Line	19/03/1917	20/03/1917
War Diary	Left Section Line of Rercstone.	20/03/1917	20/03/1917
War Diary	Old German Reserve Line	21/03/1917	21/03/1917
War Diary	Aizecourt La Haut	22/03/1917	24/03/1917
War Diary	Howitzer Wood	25/03/1917	08/04/1917
War Diary	Quinconce	09/04/1917	22/04/1917
War Diary	Equancourt	22/04/1917	24/04/1917
War Diary	Villers Plouich	25/04/1917	26/04/1917
War Diary	Etricourt	27/04/1917	30/04/1917
War Diary	Queens Cross	01/05/1917	01/05/1917
War Diary	Villers Plouich	02/05/1917	06/05/1917
War Diary	Queens Cross	06/05/1917	12/05/1917
War Diary	Line	14/05/1917	31/05/1917
War Diary	Connelieu Sector	01/06/1917	10/06/1917
War Diary	Dessart Wood	11/06/1917	19/06/1917
War Diary	Villers Plouich	19/06/1917	28/06/1917
War Diary	Fifteen Ravine	28/06/1917	30/06/1917
Miscellaneous	Headquarters 120th Bde	31/07/1917	31/07/1917
War Diary	Fifteen Ravine	01/07/1917	05/07/1917
War Diary	Villers Plouich	05/07/1917	12/07/1917
War Diary	Gouzeaucourt Trescault Road	13/07/1917	21/07/1917
War Diary	Villers Plouich	21/07/1917	29/07/1917

War Diary	Fifteen Ravine		30/07/1917	31/07/1917
War Diary			03/07/1917	21/07/1917
War Diary	15 Ravine		01/08/1917	01/08/1917
War Diary	Beaucamp		02/08/1917	02/08/1917
War Diary	15 Ravine		08/08/1917	14/08/1917
War Diary	Villers Plouich		15/08/1917	15/08/1917
War Diary	Gouzeaucourt Wood		20/08/1917	26/08/1917
War Diary	Villers Plouich		26/08/1917	31/08/1917
War Diary	Villers Plouich		25/08/1917	25/08/1917
War Diary	15 Ravine		01/09/1917	10/09/1917
War Diary	Villers Plouich		11/09/1917	11/09/1917
War Diary	Gouzeaucourt Wood		13/09/1917	13/09/1917
War Diary	Villers Plouich		19/09/1917	22/09/1917
War Diary	15 Ravine		25/09/1917	27/09/1917
War Diary	Villers Plouich		01/10/1917	08/10/1917
War Diary	Berneville		09/10/1917	29/10/1917
War Diary	Pommera		01/11/1917	11/11/1917
War Diary	Berneville		16/11/1917	16/11/1917
War Diary	Courcelles		17/11/1917	17/11/1917
War Diary	Beaulencourt		19/11/1917	19/11/1917
War Diary	Lebucquieres		21/11/1917	21/11/1917
War Diary	Hindenburg Support Line		23/11/1917	24/11/1917
War Diary	Bourlon Village		25/11/1917	30/11/1917
War Diary	Blairville		01/12/1917	01/12/1917
War Diary	Ervillers		03/12/1917	10/12/1917
War Diary	Croiselles		10/12/1917	14/12/1917
War Diary	Hindenburg Line		14/12/1917	18/12/1917
War Diary	Ervillers		18/12/1917	26/12/1917
War Diary	Croisilles		24/12/1917	27/12/1917
War Diary	Ervillers		27/12/1917	29/12/1917
War Diary	Noreuil		28/12/1917	31/12/1917
War Diary	Noreuil		01/01/1918	07/01/1918
War Diary	Mory		10/01/1918	14/01/1918
War Diary	Rt. Subsection		15/01/1918	18/01/1918
War Diary	Noreuil		18/01/1918	21/01/1918
War Diary	Rt. Subsection		22/01/1918	23/01/1918
War Diary	Rt. Subsection		22/01/1918	26/01/1918
War Diary	Mory		27/01/1918	27/01/1918
War Diary	Rt. Subsection		30/01/1918	31/01/1918
War Diary	Noreuil		01/02/1918	10/02/1918
War Diary	Mory		10/02/1918	10/02/1918
War Diary	Blairville		11/02/1918	21/02/1918
War Diary	Boisleux-Au-Mont.		22/02/1918	27/02/1918
War Diary	Pommier		28/02/1918	28/02/1918
Heading	40th Division. 120th Infantry Brigade. 14th Battalion Highland Light Infantry March 1918			
War Diary	Durham Camp		01/03/1918	01/03/1918
War Diary	Boisleaux		01/03/1918	03/03/1918
War Diary	Pommiers		03/03/1918	11/03/1918
War Diary	Ervillers		12/03/1918	21/03/1918
War Diary	Ervillers		21/03/1918	21/03/1918
War Diary	Mory		21/03/1918	21/03/1918
War Diary	Vaulx Vraucourt		22/03/1918	22/03/1918
War Diary	Army Line At Mory		22/03/1918	24/03/1918
War Diary	Behagnies		25/03/1918	25/03/1918
War Diary	Gomiecourt		25/03/1918	25/03/1918

War Diary	Ayette	25/03/1918	25/03/1918
War Diary	Adinfer Wood	26/03/1918	27/03/1918
War Diary	Warluzel	27/03/1918	29/03/1918
War Diary	Monchy Breton	29/03/1918	30/03/1918
War Diary	Sailly-Sur-La-Lys	30/03/1918	31/03/1918
Heading	40th Division. 120th Infantry Brigade. 14th Battalion The Highland Light Infantry April 1918		
War Diary	Fleurbaix	31/03/1918	06/04/1918
War Diary	Nouveau Monde	06/04/1918	09/04/1918
War Diary	Laventie	09/04/1918	09/04/1918
War Diary	Sailly Sur La Lys	09/04/1918	09/04/1918
War Diary	Le Petit Mortier	09/04/1918	10/04/1918
War Diary	A 27d	10/04/1918	11/04/1918
War Diary	Le Verrier	11/04/1918	11/04/1918
War Diary	Strazeele	12/04/1918	12/04/1918
War Diary	Pradelles	12/04/1918	13/04/1918
War Diary	Zuytpeene	14/04/1918	14/04/1918
War Diary	Tatinghem	15/04/1918	19/04/1918
War Diary	Acquin	20/04/1918	30/04/1918
War Diary	Nieurlet	01/05/1918	01/05/1918
War Diary	Rweld	02/05/1918	04/05/1918
War Diary	Watten	05/05/1918	10/05/1918
War Diary	Esquelbecq	12/05/1918	03/06/1918
War Diary	La Capelle	04/05/1918	11/05/1918
War Diary	Surques	12/05/1918	15/05/1918
War Diary	Brunembert	16/05/1918	19/07/1918
War Diary	Foufflin-Recametz	20/07/1918	31/07/1918
War Diary	Brunembert	06/07/1918	19/07/1918
Heading	66th Division Training Cadres 40 Div 120 Bde 14th Bn H.L.I. Aug-Dec 1918 1918 Aug & 1919 Apr 40 Div 120 Bde Service Will 197 Bde L of C. from Sept. 1918		
War Diary	Foufflin-Ricametz (Ref Lens II)	01/08/1918	05/08/1918
War Diary	Louches (Ref Hazebrouck) 5a	06/08/1918	15/08/1918
War Diary	Abancourt (Ref Dieppe) 16	16/08/1918	19/08/1918
War Diary	Abancourt	20/08/1918	22/08/1918
War Diary	Haudricourt (Ref Dieppe 16)	23/08/1918	31/08/1918
Heading	War Diary of 14th. Highland Light Infantry From 1st. September 1918. To 30th. September 1918 (Volume Four.)		
War Diary	Haudricourt (Ref. Dieppe 16)	01/09/1918	30/09/1918
Heading	War Diary. Of 14th. Highland Light Infantry. From 1st. October, 1918 To 31st. October, 1918 (Volume Five)		
Miscellaneous	D.A.G., G.H.Q., 3rd. Echelon.	01/11/1918	01/11/1918
War Diary	Haudricourt (Ref Dieppe 16)	01/10/1918	31/10/1918
Heading	War Diary of 14th. Highland Light Infantry. From 1st. November, 1918. To 30th. November. 1918 Volume Five.		
War Diary	Haudricourt (Ref. Dieppe 16)	01/11/1918	10/12/1918
War Diary	Havre	11/12/1918	31/12/1918
Heading	Training Cadre 39th Division Divl Troops 197 Bde 66 Division 14th Bn High'd Lt Infy Jan-Apr 1919		
War Diary		01/01/1919	31/01/1919
War Diary	Le Havre	01/02/1919	30/04/1919

26/9/2 (1)
9:06am

26/9/2 (11)
9:50am

40TH DIVISION
120TH INFY BDE

14TH BN HIGH'D LT INFY.

JUN 1916-JLY 1918

Confidential.

War Diary

of the

14ᵗʰ (S) Bn Highland Light Infantry.

from 3ʳᵈ June 1916 to 30ᵗʰ June 1916.

Volume I. (Commencement of Record.)

G.H.Crawford Lieut & Adjutant
14ᵗʰ Bn H.L.I.

Army Form C. 2118

WAR DIARY
~~INTELLIGENCE SUMMARY~~
(Erase heading not required.)

Place	Date	Hour	Summary of Events and Information	Remarks and references to Appendices
BLACKDOWN	3.6.16		The Battalion marched from Deffinger Barracks to FARNBOROUGH STATION. L.S.W. Rly where it entrained in two trains and proceeded to SOUTHAMPTON, remaining in the sheds in the docks until the evening when it embarked on S.S. CAESAREA. The transport animals and personnel embarked on S.S.	
HAVRE	4.6.16		The Battalion disembarked at HAVRE and marched to No 2 Rest Camp where it remained until the evening of 5.-6.-16	
HAVRE	5.6.16		The Battalion entrained at HAVRE at 9 p.m. leaving at 11.30 p.m.	
LILLERS	6.6.16		The Battalion disentrained at LILLERS at 7 p.m. and marched to ECQUEDECQUES where it remained in rest billets until 11.6.16	
ECQUEDECQUES	11.6.16	8 a.m	The Battalion marched at 8 a.m to BETHUNE where it billeted for the night	
BETHUNE	12.6.16		The Battalion moved off by Companies for instructional purposes. Companies attached as follows: Division for instructional purposes. Companies attached to the 46th Inf Bde 15th A Coy to 7/8 K.O.S.B's. B Coy to 10/11 H.L.I. C to 12. H.L.I. D Coy to 10th Scottish Rifles. Batt HQ to Batt HQ 7/8 K.O.S.B's.	

H Crawford 2/Lt
14 HLI

Army Form C. 2118

WAR DIARY
INTELLIGENCE SUMMARY
(Erase heading not required.)

Instructions regarding War Diaries and Intelligence Summaries are contained in F. S. Regs., Part II. and the Staff Manual respectively. Title Pages will be prepared in manuscript.

Place	Date	Hour	Summary of Events and Information	Remarks and references to Appendices
In the Trenches.	12-6-16 to 16-6-16		The Batt? has attacked as shown on Sheet 1. during this period. from reports received from the various battalions, to which Companies were attached, the men gave great satisfaction both in the manner in which they carried out any duties they have been called upon to perform and also in their conduct under fire. The weather during this period was very bad and the trenches were in a very bad condition. The test for the men & troops was therefore somewhat severe.	
ANNEQUIN.	16-6-16 to 20-6-16		The Battalion withdrew from the trenches on 16th 6.16 and remained in rest billets at ANNEQUIN.	
	20-6-16 to 23-6-16		The Battalion has attacks for instruction in Coy Training in ANNEQUIN. 45th Brigade. Batt? H.Q. remained in ANNEQUIN. Companies were attacked as follows:— A Coy. to 6/7th Royal Scots Fusiliers B Coy. to 13th R? Royal Scots. C Coy to 6th Cameron Highlanders D Coy to 11th B? A & S.H.	

Crawford 2Lt adj.
14/6 H.D.

Army Form C. 2118

WAR DIARY
INTELLIGENCE SUMMARY
(Erase heading not required.)

Place	Date	Hour	Summary of Events and Information	Remarks and references to Appendices
Trenches.	21-6-16		On the evening of 21st June at 2ɸ o'clock a mine was blown up opposite the sub section held by the 6th Cameron Highlanders. C Coy 14th H.L.I. attacked to their left. Battalion was ordered to occupy the lip of the crater. The disposition's made by Captain Shepherd commanding the Coy proved entirely satisfactory, and the crater was occupied but four casualties, and held by the Coy until they quitted the trenches on 23rd inst.	
ANNEQUIN	23-6-16		The Batt'n. withdrew to billets at ANNEQUIN and remained there for the night. The total casualties during both periods of attachment were 5 other ranks killed and 11 other ranks wounded.	
Annequin	24-6-16		The Battalion marched at 8 A.M. to BRUAY where the 120th Brigade were being collected together after their period of attachment for instructional purposes. Battalion again in billets.	
BRUAY	25-6-16 to 30-6-16		The Battalion remained in billets at BRUAY during this period — The training being confined to attacks from trenches — consolidating craters — Route Marching — Special attention being given to bombing and wiring	

E.C. Manford Lt/Col
14th H.L.I.

WAR DIARY
INTELLIGENCE SUMMARY

Place	Date	Hour	Summary of Events and Information	Remarks and references to Appendices
BRUAY	27.6.16		On this date Captain J.G. Clemens, Adjutant, left the Battalion to take up a new appointment as Brigade Major to the 141st Brigade – 2/Lieut G.C. Manford assumed the duties of adjutant –	
"	28.6.16		The following reinforcements of officers were received. – Lieut E.G.S. Gordon 10th W.Y.1 2nd A.Y. Hutchison 13th W.Y.1 2/Lieut G.H. Haydock 13th " " W.R.C. Carmichael 13th " " R. Haddock 13th "	
BRUAY	28.6.16		On this date the Battalion were still in billets at BRUAY.	

John Crawford Stack
14th W.Y.I.

40 of July

14 H.L.
Vol 2

2.N.
4 sheets

Government
War Fund
14 (8) Ivo Aylwens light Infantry
VOLUME 2 (July 1914)

WAR DIARY / INTELLIGENCE SUMMARY

Army Form C. 2118

Place	Date	Hour	Summary of Events and Information	Remarks and references to Appendices
BRUAY	1/7/16		Battalion remain in billets at BRUAY	
BRUAY	4/7/16	7.30 am	Battalion left BRUAY & marched to LES BREBIS where it was quartered in Billets as the Brigade being in Divisional Reserve till the 11th of July.	
LES BREBIS	11/7/16	10.30 hours	The Brigade relieved the 142nd Brigade in the line - The Battalion relieved the 20th Bn. MIDDLESEX Regt in Brigade Reserve & were quartered in NORTH MAROC. The relief was completed by 22-20 hours. Only 20 officers actually were taken into the line.	
NORTH MAROC	14/7/16		The Battalion remained in B'de Reserve for four days, situation was normal during this period. Working parties under the R.E. were supplied every night & during the day three working parties under an officer were employed in repairing the Reserve line & communication trenches from the Reserve line to the Support line. Lieut A.W. Gill toured the R's from the base.	
NORTH MAROC	15/7/16	9 hours	The Battalion commenced relieving the 13th Bn. East Surrey Regt. in the Right Sub-section of the MAROC section - the relief was completed by 14-35 hours. The wire appears to be very weak on the front of this subsection & wiring parties were working most of the night strengthening it.	
In the Trenches	16/7/16		Situation normal. Working parties by day & night repairing the trenches & strengthening wire - the front was patrolled during this night, nothing of importance was reported.	
LES BREBIS	17/7/16		The Bn. was relieved by the 20th MIDDLESEX Regt. The relief was completed by 9 hours. The Bn. on completion of relief marched by Platoons to LES BREBIS where it was quartered in Billets, the Brigade being in Divisional Reserve.	

Charles Major for Lt Col
Commdg 11th R.W.S.

Army Form C. 2118

WAR DIARY
or
INTELLIGENCE SUMMARY
(Erase heading not required.)

Place	Date	Hour	Summary of Events and Information	Remarks and references to Appendices
LES BREBIS	18.7.16 to 22.7.16		Battn. remained in LES BREBIS & supplied working parties.	
CALONNE	22.7.16		The Brigade relieved the 119th Inf Bde in the Calonne section. The 10th H.L.I relieved the 10th Welsh Regt who went in Bde support - were billeted in Calonne. Working parties were supplied to the R.E. & the section g defences improved. The element of little advance was received & it was decided that the two Coys holding the village were not to be taken for working parties outside this area.	
	27.7.16		A Coy relieved Coy 13th S. Surrey Regt in the front line. 2 O.R. killed by rifle grenade.	
CALONNE	30.7.16		Battn. was relieved by 14th Bn. WELSH Regt & proceeded to BULLY GRENAY where it was quartered in Billets & formed the Bn. in Brigade Reserve to the 119th Brigade holding the CALONNE section of the defences. Relief was completed at 21 hours.	

Churton Mayor Lt H.Col
Commdg 14. 8. 19

WAR DIARY

3.N.

1/4th (S) Bn
Highland Light Infantry

August 1916

VOLUME 3

WAR DIARY or INTELLIGENCE SUMMARY

Army Form C. 2118

Place	Date	Hour	Summary of Events and Information	Remarks and references to Appendices
BULLY GRENAY	1.8.16		Batt. remains in billets.	
	2.8.16		Major C. Harlan hands to take command of the 2nd Batt.	
	3.8.16		120 of Inf. Bug. relieves the 171st Inf. Bug. at 100 S.	
100 S	4.8.16		14th H.L.I. relieves the 2nd Middlesex in No 3 Sub-section. Relief unopposed. Fairly quiet. 1. O.R. killed.	
	5.8.16		T.M. active. 8.O.R. wounded.	
	6.8.16		T.M. very active. 1.O.R. killed. 12.O.R. wounded.	
	7.8.16		1.O.R. killed. 5.O.R. wounded.	
	8.8.16		Front line trenches in very bad state especially between HARTS CRATER & B9 A40 35. 2nd 7ths fail to keep down enemy fire. 120 of Inf. Bug. relieved by 47 Inf. Bug. 14th H.L.I. relieved by 7th Sinaforth. 6th Royal West Rifles, 8 Connaughts. 1.O.R. killed. 3.O.R. wounded.	
	9.8.16		The Batt. moves to MAROC & occupies billets for the night.	
MAROC	10.8.16		The Batt. takes over the line from the 6th Welsh - EDWARE ROAD to LIVERPOOL STREET. LIEUT GORDON leaves for R.F.C. L.2.R killed 4.O.R wounded	

WAR DIARY or INTELLIGENCE SUMMARY

Army Form C. 2118

Place	Date	Hour	Summary of Events and Information	Remarks and references to Appendices
MAROC	11.8.16		CAPT F.L. PATON wounded (slight) 1 O.R. wounded	
	12.8.16		121st Bng. relieves 120th Bng. 2.O.R. wounded. 10th Suffolks relieve 14th H.L.I. Relief complete by 5.30 p.m.	
LES BREBIS	12.8.16 to 16.8.16		The Batt. occupies "D" billets in LES BREBIS	
	16.8.16		119th Inf. Bng. is relieved by 120th Inf. Bng. 12th S.W.B. are relieved by 14th H.L.I. who are in support. Relief complete by 6.15 p.m.	
CALONNE	16.8.16 to 20.8.16		The Batt. is in support in CALONNE	
	20.8.16		The Batt: relieves the 12th E. Surrey Regt in the Right Sub-Section CALONNE BOYAUX 200 (exc) to 219 (in)	
	21.8.16		Enemy wire cut at M.21.a.05.70 by Right Group D.A. Very well done. 2/Lt Carmichael makes a reconnaissance of the position.	
	22.8.16	10.15 p.m.	A raiding party under 2/Lts Carmichael & Stevenson with 20 O.R. left our front line with German trench at M.21.a.05.70 as objective. [2. O.R wounded.]	

WAR DIARY
or
INTELLIGENCE SUMMARY

Army Form C. 2118

Place	Date	Hour	Summary of Events and Information	Remarks and references to Appendices
CALONNE	22.6.16	10.50 P.M.	ZERO time the Right Group D.A. opened its Barrage. At this moment 2/Lt CARMICHAEL approached though the gap cut by the artillery to within 25 yds of the centre of his objective. He at once rushed into the trench where there was a working party of 10 or 12 Germans, of whom he killed one & wounded another with his revolver. The casualties were undoubtedly inflicted by our bombs. At the same time, covering party of 2/Lt STEVENSON, 5 O.R. deployed at about 30 yds from the sap head. They moved 2/Lt CARMICHAELS party got into the sap. They moved off to the left towards the sap-head. The rear party moving down to the junction of sap & trench. Perhaps caused great dash with the bayonet. The wounded German was found & lifted over the parapet.	
	23.6.16	12.10 A.M.	2/Lt CARMICHAEL remembers our trenches, but immediately goes out again with 2/Lt STEVENSON to look for the s...	J.H.Tulloch Major 1/4 R.H.V.

Army Form C. 2118

WAR DIARY
or
INTELLIGENCE SUMMARY
(Erase heading not required.)

Place	Date	Hour	Summary of Events and Information	Remarks and references to Appendices
CALONNE	23/8/16		of the party who were still unaccounted for. After making two separate journeys, they were all brought in, with the exception of 1 N.C.O. (missing)	
	22.8.16		Patrol under 2/Lt Burton took out Bangalore Torpedo & placed it in German wire opposite PICT AXE SAP.	
		11.17 P.M	It was successfully fired by the R.E. at 11.17 P.M. Bugles no wire no signal – could not be heard. Much valuable information was obtained from the prisoner. The success of the operation was due to:– 1. Carefully thought out plan, after thorough reconnaissance. 2. Clear & detailed orders issued by the C.O. 3. Gallantry & reckless daring & fine leadership of 2/Lt Carmichael 4. Close cooperation of artillery. Raid casualties. 1 O.R. killed. 10.R. missing 4 O.R. wounded.	

J. H. Joule Major
1/4 K. H. L. I.

WAR DIARY

Army Form C. 2118

Place	Date	Hour	Summary of Events and Information	Remarks and references to Appendices
BULLY GRENAY	24/8/16		12th Batt. East Surrey Regt. relieves the 14th H.L.I. Relief completed by 9.30 A.M. 2/Lt MATHIESON, D. 2/Lt GILL, A.W. wounded. The Batt. goes into Brigade Reserve & occupies billets in BULLY GRENAY	
	25/8/16		Lieut H. BROWN reported for duty. No.29487 Pte SMITH, E. awarded military medal for the following act of gallantry:— When telephonic communication was broken with the Right Coy at LOOS, he remained on duty for 39 hours & refused the Coy at LOOS, he volunteered for this duty & refused to be relieved. The lines had to be laid across the open as the trench was blown in. Under a heavy bombardment he succeeded single handed in laying a new system of wires.	
LES BREBIS	30.8.16		The Batt. was relieved by the 13th Royal Fusiliers. The Batt. moves to LES BREBIS & occupies billets in "I" area, the Brigade being in Divisional Reserve.	

J.H. Stoter Major
14th H.L.I.

VOLUME 4

14th H.L.I. (glasgow Highland) 1st Bn.

WAR DIARY
INTELLIGENCE SUMMARY

Army Form C. 2118

H.N.
3 sheets

Place	Date	Hour	Summary of Events and Information	Remarks and references to Appendices
LES BREBIS	1.9.16 to 5.9.16		The Batt remains in Billets at LES BREBIS. 120th Bde relieves the 121st Bde. Batt relieves 2nd Middlesex Regt in the Right Subsector Maroc.	
Maroc	5.9.16		Very quiet - retaliation futile. Casualties 5.9.16 to 17.9.16 3 O.R. killed 9 O.R. wounded	
	6.9.16		2nd Lieut Ian Carmichael awarded D.S.O. 2nd Lieut J.H. Stevenson awarded M.C. Military Medals are awarded to	
	9.9.16		Cpl. R.D. Ballantyne, 2/Lt A. Katt, 2/Lt R. Munro 2/Lt G.H. Hancock. Hence the Batt Capt. Ballantyne O.C. 'B' Coy Capt. Nicolson returned from Bde. 2/Lt D.B. Warren goes to 104th Bde.	
	12.9.16		Batt relieved by 13th E. Surrey Regt & goes into Brigade Reserve in Y.E. Maroc.	
	19.9.16		Batt relieved by 19th R. Welsh Fusiliers 119th Inf Bde. Batt goes into Div Reserve at PETIT SAINS	

Army Form C. 2118

WAR DIARY
or
INTELLIGENCE SUMMARY
(Erase heading not required.)

Place	Date	Hour	Summary of Events and Information	Remarks and references to Appendices
PETIT SAINS	19.9.16 to 22.9.16		Batt in Billets at PETIT SAINS.	
	21.9.16		C.O. goes on leave.	
LOOS 14 BIS	22.9.16		120th Inf Bgde relieves 78th Inf Bde in the 14 Bde(Loos) Section. Batt relieves 2nd Suffolks in the R. Subsection. A few casualties during relief - communication trenches not dug enough. Trenches in bad condition - little work had been done on them. Fairly quiet - casualties caused by rifle grenades. Casualties during tour: 3 O.R. Killed. 14 O.R. wounded. Most of them slight. Batt relieved by 11 H.K.R. go down onto Brigade Reserve at Mazingarbe.	
MAZINGARBE	26.9.16			
	27.9.16		Capt Coles returns from Rest Camp.	
	28.9.16		Capt Hanford returns from leave & goes to the 119 K. Brig office for a course.	

J H Foster, Major
14/K/R/L

WAR DIARY
or
INTELLIGENCE SUMMARY
(Erase heading not required.)

Army Form C. 2118

Place	Date	Hour	Summary of Events and Information	Remarks and references to Appendices
14 Bis	30/11/16		The Battn. relieved the 11th King's Own R. Lancaster Regt in the Right Subsection. Relief complete 11.55 A.M. Enemy extraordinarily quiet. Capt. Blackledge returns from leave. J.H. Jarvis Major 14th K.L.R.	

WAR DIARY

OCTOBER
————
VOL 5

11th Highland Light Infantry

VOLUME 5
————

5N.
6 sheets

Army Form C. 2118

WAR DIARY
or
~~INTELLIGENCE SUMMARY~~

(Erase heading not required.)

Instructions regarding War Diaries and Intelligence Summaries are contained in F.S. Regs., Part II. and the Staff Manual respectively. Title Pages will be prepared in manuscript.

Place	Date	Hour	Summary of Events and Information	Remarks and references to Appendices
RIGHT SUBSEC. 14.BIS.	3.10.16.		2nd Lieut Ritchie took out small party with a Bangala Torpedo, Torpedo failed to explode, they afterwards went out and brought back the unexploded torpedo.	
VILLAGE LINE 14.BIS.	4.10.16		Batt. relieved by 11th K.O.R.L. & goes into support in village line, relief complete by 12 Noon. Transfer Very Lad. CO returns from Leave.	
	7.10.16		CO goes to 1st Army School at Boulogne for Conference.	
RIGHT Subsect 14.BIS.	8.10.16		Batt. relieves 11th K.O.R.L. in its R Subsection 14.BIS. relief complete 2.40 PM.	
	10.10.16		2nd Lieuts C. RAMSEY & 2nd Lieut N.M.CLARK Reported for duty with Batt. and posted to A & C Coys respectively. ENEMY Very quiet.	
PHILOSOPHE.	12.10.16.		14th H.L.I relieved by the 21st Mdx reg. and went into Brigade Reserve billets at PHILOSOPHE. relief complete 10.30 A.M.	
	15.10.16		Extract from the GAZETTE of 10.10.16 H.L.I TEMP CAPT H.T. COLES to be TEMP MAJOR 3 Aug 1916. TEMP CAPT G.C. MANFORD to be ADJUTANT 27 JUNE 1916. The undermentioned to be TEMP CAPT. TEMP. 2nd Lieut R.D BLACKLEDGE. 28th JUNE 1916. TEMP LIEUT N. MACHINNON. 3 Aug 1916. The UNDERMENTIONED TEMP 2nd LIEUTS to be TEMP LIEUTS. W.N. LOWE 4th JUNE 1916. C.G. RITCHIE 3rd Aug 1916.	

Army Form C. 2118

WAR DIARY
or
INTELLIGENCE SUMMARY
(Erase heading not required.)

Instructions regarding War Diaries and Intelligence Summaries are contained in F.S. Regs., Part II. and the Staff Manual respectively. Title Pages will be prepared in manuscript.

Place	Date	Hour	Summary of Events and Information	Remarks and references to Appendices
PHILOSOPHE.	16.10.16		C.O. Returns from Conference at Boulogne. Major Anderson 19th H.L.I attached for instruction.	
	17.10.16		Corps Commander inspected Billets. Improvements to Billets.	
RIGHT SUBSECTION HULLUCH	18.10.16		14th H.L.I. relieved 11th K.O.R.L. in the Right Subsection Hulluch relief complete at 12.15 PM. Enemy's wire reconnoitred for projected raid.	
	20.10.16		Major Foster goes on leave. Sir R. West Kent officers reconnoitred the line preparatory to relieving the 14th H.L.I. in the Right Subsection Hulluch.	
	21.10.16		An enemy heavy T.M. reported firing for the first time on our front line slight damage done. Enemy's Aerial Dart-Batteries made active relief suspected. Enemy's heavy T.M. caused large amount of damage to our front line & support Lieut. J.B. Beveridge the signalling officer killed whilst superintending the laying of telephone wires to centre Coy's H.Q. about 5 P.M. N Killed by heavy T.M. in a dug-out in the front line at head of salient in 14.19.?	
	22.10.16	7 PM	A Raid consisting of 1 Officer and 50.O.R was made on the Enemy's front line in 14.19.? for the purpose of gaining identifications. 2 Parties, one led by Lieut. C.G. Ritchie and the other by Sergeant H. Anglin, entered the enemy trenches through 2 gaps in the wire previously cut by the Artillery, covered by our Artillery Barrage on either flank and on the enemy's support line. Both Parties found the enemy very alert and	

1875. Wt. W593/826. 1,000,000 4/15 J.B.C. & A. A.D.S.S./Forms/C. 2118.

WAR DIARY
or
~~INTELLIGENCE SUMMARY~~

(Erase heading not required.)

Army Form C. 2118

Place	Date	Hour	Summary of Events and Information	Remarks and references to Appendices
RIGHT SUBSECTION HULLUCH.	22.10.16		Passed on if about to Raid our trenches. Both parties engaged in a bombing fight with the enemy but eventually had to withdraw as the enemy was in greater strength. Lt RITCHIE was wounded by machine gun fire and bomb splinters early in the operation and was carried back to our trenches by L/Corp ROBERTS and PRIVATE McLACHLAN. Sergeant ANGLIS extricated his party with great skill back to our trenches. We were unable to obtain any identifications, but a rifle was brought back by Pte FERGUSON a diminutive soldier who afterwards related that he had ripped it out of a German's hands and bayoneted him with his own weapon. Our Casualties were 1 OFFICER Wounded, 6 OR slightly wounded and 5 missing (3 believed killed).	
	23.10.16		ENEMY Heavy T.M. with very active and considerable damage done to trenches. 2nd Lieut Coles, 253rd TUNNELLING Coy. R.E with a party of sappers came with assistance of the central Coy to help rescue the men who had been entombed the night before. Their times were driven away by heavy T.M. and arrived das pin as the place where they were working was under observation from the enemy and only about 60yds from	

1875 Wt. W593/826 1,000,000 4/15 J.B.C. & A. A.D.S.S./Forms/C. 2118.

WAR DIARY or INTELLIGENCE SUMMARY

Army Form C. 2118

(Erase heading not required.)

Place	Date	Hour	Summary of Events and Information	Remarks and references to Appendices
RIGHT SUBSECTION AULLOCH	23.10.16 24.10.16		The ENEMY'S front line. at about 4 AM on the morning of the 24.10.16, 5 men were reported alive; during the operation 3 sappers were killed, I RE S/r killed and 2 sappers wounded. 2nd Lieut COLE'S worked with great gallantry during all this heavy work. LIEUT H BROWN Slightly wounded, Carried dusk.	
LES BREBIS	25.10.16		14th H.L.I. Relieved by 8th R. WEST KENT'S relief complete 12. Noon. and went into Billets at LES BREBIS.	
	26.10.16		Draft 100 MEN Received, CAPT MANFORD Returned from 19th BRIG. The following officers joined for duty with Batt and posted as under. 2nd Lieut HODGE POSTED TO C. COY. " S. LEEKIE " B. " " J.C. PRATT " D. " " J HOUSTON " B. " " J ORR " D. " " G SOUTAR " D. " " J CARMICHAEL. D.S.O. Rejoined A.COY. 2nd Lieut C. W HARDIE Transferred to 120th M.G. COY.	
BRUAY La THIEULOYE	27.10.16 28.10.16		BATT. moved at 8. 30 AM by MARCH ROUTE to BRUAY and went into Billets. arrived 11PM. BATT moved at 8.45 AM by MARCH ROUTE to La THIEULOYE and went into Billets arrived 12.40 PM	
BAILLEUL aux CORNAILLES	29.10.16		Batt moved at 10.30 AM by MARCH ROUTE to BAILLEUL aux CORNAILLES and went into Billets. arrived 12.30 PM	

Army Form C. 2118

WAR DIARY
or
INTELLIGENCE SUMMARY
(Erase heading not required.)

Instructions regarding War Diaries and Intelligence Summaries are contained in F. S. Regs., Part II. and the Staff Manual respectively. Title Pages will be prepared in manuscript.

Place	Date	Hour	Summary of Events and Information	Remarks and references to Appendices
BAILLEUL AUX CORNAILLES	30/10/16		Batt route march & Coy training.	
	31/10/16		Major Forbes returned off leave. Major Anderson attached for instruction left for 24th Division. Total Casualties for month. 1 Officer Killed. 2 wounded O.R. 9 Killed 9 Missing 33 wounded.	

H. A. Palm Major
In Comd 14th H.L.I.

1st Hatfield Rfls [?]

WAR DIARY
or
INTELLIGENCE SUMMARY

Army Form C. 2118

Vol 6

6. N.
5 sheets

Place	Date	Hour	Summary of Events and Information	Remarks and references to Appendices
BAILLEUL and CORBAHUR	1.11.16		Brigade tactical exercise on Lewis guns in attack & defence. Batt. starts in the afternoon.	
CANETTEMONT	2.11.16		Batt. marched to CANETTEMONT and HONVAL & eventually billets very wet then badly in need of repair - new ones issued, being of very poor material. C.O. inspects all companies. Capt Bingham goes on leave.	
	3.11.16		Batt. left CANETTEMONT at 8 A.M. and marched to VILLERS L'HOPITAL - arrived 11.30 A.M. - roads bad in places - fine.	
VILLERS L'HOPITAL	4.11.16		Batt. VILLERS L'HOPITAL at 8 A.M. & marched to BERNAVILLE - arrived 11 A.M. - no men fell out. Roads fair but hilly.	
BERNAVILLE	5.11.16		Batt. practises trench attack - met - concert.	
	7.11.16		The Corps Commander awards the Military Medal to :- No 23774 Pte WILLIAM FERGUSSON for the following act of gallantry :- On the night of the 22/23 Oct 1916 Pte FERGUSSON formed part of a raiding party which penetrated the German front line. Pte FERGUSSON is a small man ;	

WAR DIARY
or
INTELLIGENCE SUMMARY
(Erase heading not required.)

Army Form C. 2118

Place	Date	Hour	Summary of Events and Information	Remarks and references to Appendices
BERNAFAY	7.11.16		when the two he snatched a rifle (with fixed bayonet) from a big German, emerging from a dug-out, the bayonet the German with his short weapon — killing him on the spot, as he found himself unable to extract the bayonet, he unlocked it, whereupon the German fell down the steps of the dug-out with his own bayonet inside him. Four hours later Pte FERGUSSON handed in the German rifle & experienced regret that he had been unable to obtain identification of his victim. Pte FERGUSSON showed great coolness both before & after the above incident.	
			Coy. Parades	
	8.11.16		Batt Musketry trench attack	
	9.11.16		Brigade Field Day — Artillery formation.	
	10.11.16		Coy Parades	
	11.11.16		The G.O.C. in C. awarded the D.C.M. to :- No 29612 Sgt HAWKINS for the following act of gallantry :-	

WAR DIARY or INTELLIGENCE SUMMARY

Army Form C. 2118

Place	Date	Hour	Summary of Events and Information	Remarks and references to Appendices
BERNAVILLE	11.11.18		At 7 P.M. on the 22nd Oct 1918 Sergt Hughes led a raiding party of 14 O.R. through the gap in the German wire & found the French full of Germans. He bombed into the trench killed two & when overwhelmed by numbers conducted the retirement of his party in a most able manner. He carried back himself, the only wounded man of his party. After being so he returned to "no-mans-land" & was out for two hours under heavy fire searching for wounded of the raiding party into that gone out on his night simultaneously with his own.	
DOULLENS	12.11.18		Batt. marches to DOULLENS via FIENVILLERS and HEM & goes into billets. Reached S.H.S at 8 A.M.	
SOUASTRE	13.11.16		Batt. parades at 9 A.M. & marches to SOUASTRE – arrived 12.15. P.M.	
	14.11.16		2 P.M. the Batt. becomes Brigade Reserve to the 148th Inf. Brig. The Batt. marches to HEBUTERNE & is billeted in the outskirts. The Batt. relieves the 94 York's Lancs Regt. & is in SUPPORT.	

WAR DIARY
or
INTELLIGENCE SUMMARY

(Erase heading not required.)

Army Form C. 2118

Place	Date	Hour	Summary of Events and Information	Remarks and references to Appendices
HEBUTERNE	18.11.16 / 19.11.16		Batt. comes under 31st Division. Batt. works on HEBUTERNE defences. Improvement of trenches & wiring.	
COIGNEUX	20.11.16		The Batt. is relieved by the 13th Batt. W. Yorkshire Regt & marches to billets in COIGNEUX - camp very muddy.	
	21.11.16		The Batt. marches to a camp in the BOIS DE WARNIMONT - huts very bad & camp very muddy.	
AMPLIER	22.11.16		Batt. marches to billets in AMPLIER.	
FIEFFES	23.11.16		Batt. marches to billets in FIEFFES and CRAMPEES - fine roads good.	
GORENFLOS	24.11.16		Batt. marches to billets in GORENFLOS - only two men fell out of the march, many had worn out boots & their feet were sore. Individual training commences. C.O.C. presents D.C.M to Sergt Anglim.	

Army Form C. 2118

WAR DIARY
or
INTELLIGENCE SUMMARY
(Erase heading not required.)

Instructions regarding War Diaries and Intelligence Summaries are contained in F.S. Regs., Part II. and the Staff Manual respectively. Title Pages will be prepared in manuscript.

Place	Date	Hour	Summary of Events and Information	Remarks and references to Appendices

GOREN FLOS	28.11.16 to 30.11.16		Individual training.
			
			Casualties during the month
			    2 O.R. killed
			    1 O.R. wounded.
			
			2/Lt. H.C. Black reported for duty 22.11.16
			2/Lt. H. Fraser " " " 28.11.16
			2/Lt. S.D. Johnston " " " "
			
			The 40th Division came under 15th Corps 5th Army.
			
			            J.H. Stokes, Major
			            14.H.H.L.I.	

Army Form C. 2118

WAR DIARY
or INTELLIGENCE SUMMARY
(Erase heading not required.)

Vol 7

Place	Date	Hour	Summary of Events and Information	Remarks and references to Appendices
GORENFLOS	1.12.16 to 13.12.16		Individual & Company training. Junior Officers under Brigade Majors. Crying Barrage practised. Capt Manford goes sick.	
	13.12.16		The Batt: marches to ST ETOILE & were billeted for the night.	
ST ETOILE	14.12.16		Till 40 th Div. two hundred entrains at CONDÉ & detrains at EDGEHILL (BUIRE SUR L'ANCRE). The 11th H.L.I. & 11th K. R. Rifles march to CAMP 13.	
CAMP 13	15.12.16		2/Lt D.B. WARREN takes over the duties of Adjutant. Camp very muddy. Huts poor. Volume made out for improvement of camp & work carried on.	
	16.12.16 to 23.12.16			
	23.12.16		C.O. & Coy Commanders reconnoitred Reft. Subsection BOUCHAVESNES NORTH. Batt: moves to Camp 111 arrives at 11.30 AM. C.O. Lunches with G.O.C. 120th Inf. Brig. proceeded by Commanding Officers conference.	
CAMP 111	24.12.16			
	25.12.16		Cinema entertainment to men by 4th Div.	

Army Form C. 2118

WAR DIARY
or
INTELLIGENCE SUMMARY
(Erase heading not required.)

Instructions regarding War Diaries and Intelligence Summaries are contained in F.S. Regs., Part II. and the Staff Manual respectively. Title Pages will be prepared in manuscript.

Place	Date	Hour	Summary of Events and Information	Remarks and references to Appendices
CAMP III BOUCHAVESNES NORTH	26.12.16		Batt. left Camp III at 1.45PM in Motor Lorries and proceeded to MAUREPAS, itinue guides to TRENCHES. LEFT SUBSECTION NORTH BOUCHAVESNES. C coy on right. D on left. B in support. A Coy in reserve at ANDOVER PLACE. Guides with leading 3 platoons and H.Q's went wrong and delayed relief. Relief complete at 1.15 A.M. Very bad night (raining) trenches very bad.	
"	27.12.16		C.O. and 2M in command went round whole front line system of trenches, men seemed quite cheerful. Left Coy trenches good but right Coy's support Coy very bad. Communication trench had 2 to 2½ feet of water in parts. 1 man wounded. Batt. H.Q. to have line improved. Enemy shells in little bunches across the open which resulted in missing an enemy shell in intermittent shelling during day. A quiet day Coys relieved at night. B Coy going to right A Coy into left. C coy to support and D Coy to reserve.	
"	28.12.16		Left and conditions of trenches again very bad health of men recovering slightly. Snow, almost impossible to do any work on them.	J H Twitley Lt Col

WAR DIARY
or
INTELLIGENCE SUMMARY
(Erase heading not required.)

Army Form C. 2118

Place	Date	Hour	Summary of Events and Information	Remarks and references to Appendices
NORTH BOUCHAVESNES	29.12.16		A fairly quiet day. C.O. & 3 Coy Commanders 20th Middlesex arrived to reconnoitre the line.	
	30.12.16		The thin front line Coys relieved by 13th East Surreys relief started at 5:30 PM completed at 9:30 PM. The Coy in reserve or another place remained under orders of 13th East Surreys. HQ. and A.B. & C. Coys proceeded to ASQUITH FLATS as Batt. in Support together with 1 Coy of 14th A & S.H. The journey back was very trying owing to the mud 35 minute alone being spent in getting on our own way to the field. Finally arrived at ASQUITH FLATS AT 2AM on 31.12.16. All men accommodated in dug out. H.Q. dug out very wet.	
ASQUITH FLATS	31.12.16		Batt relieved by 21st Middlesex. (the 120th Brigade being relieved by 121st Brigade) relief complete at 6:30 PM Batt marched by Coys to MAUREPAS and then taken by Motor Lorries to CAMP 17. The 120th BRIGADE Becoming Brigade in reserve.	Major [signature] 31.12.16
CAMP 17.			TOTAL CASUALTIES FOR MONTH 5 OR KILLED 17 OR WOUNDED.	

WAR DIARY
or
INTELLIGENCE SUMMARY

Army Form C. 2118

Place	Date	Hour	Summary of Events and Information	Remarks and references to Appendices
CAMP 17 SUZANNE SUR SOMME	1.1.17		All men resting after relief	
	2.1.17 to 3.1.17		Batt refitting for a much tour in trenches. CAPT R.G. BLACKLEDGE receives MILITARY CROSS IN NEW YEAR'S Honours LIST MAJOR J.H. FOSTER proceeds to England to attend senior officers course at ALDERSHOT. Lt. COL. DICK D.S.O. went sick and sent down to C.C.S. MAJOR H.P. COLES took over temp. command of Batt. Batt moves at 11.0c from Camp 17 and proceeded to MAOREPAS RAVINE by MOTOR LORRIES to relieve 119th S.W.B. in BRIGADE RESERVE. relief completed 12.45 P.M. batt became Brigade reserve. (120th INF BRIGADE relieved 19th INF BRIGADE RANCOURT SECTOR.) Men live in tents and dug outs. 2nd Lt M.H. GRAY ? struck off strength evacuated to ENGLAND. Lt. H.BROWN.	
MAOREPAS RAVINE	4.1.17			
	6.1.17		men employed in clearing up Camp and fatigues. Lt. Col. DICK D.S.O & 2nd Lt. I CARMICHAEL mentioned in dispatches (New year honour list). Lt. Col Dick D.S.O. returns from C.C.S. and took on command of Batt.	
	7.1.17		Major Coles and two front company commanders reconnoitred left half front RANCOURT, preparatory to taking over from 13th E. Surrey's.	

WAR DIARY
or
INTELLIGENCE SUMMARY

Army Form C. 2118

Place	Date	Hour	Summary of Events and Information	Remarks and references to Appendices
MAUREPAS RAVINE. RANCOURT.	8.1.17		Left Maurepas ravine at 4.0 P.M. Relieved 13th E. Surreys in left sub section RANCOURT. Relief complete 9.30 P.M. Quiet night.	
RANCOURT.	9.1.17		INTERMITTENT SHELLING during day, otherwise all quiet. 2Lt COLQUHADICK D.S.O. left Bn to go on leave from 10th Jan — 20th Jan. Major Lt P. COLES took on command of Batt. VISIT from MAJOR GENERAL INTER COY Relief. Coys going up to front line took 48 hrs rations with them to save carrying up on 3rd night. Relief very satisfactory. Intermittent shelling heavy at times but no casualties. R.S.M. W. J. SHEPHERD receives D.C.M. (New Years honours list). 2nd Lt. G.E.13. MCINDOE up all [?] daily Patrol to A Coy but remain with details at Camp 20.	
"	10.1.17			
"	11.1.17		B.G.G.S. 15th CORPS VISITED. It's during morning with G.S.O.I. 48th Div took a Par Lim Post being carried out as much as possible. Duck board sent up, all posts are now practically dry. Telephone Line laid to left and right Coys during night 10th/11th. 2/D Batt Coy now in Communication with Batt H.Q. Rather more shelling than usual, especially at night, one post blown in at a few casualties.	

WAR DIARY or INTELLIGENCE SUMMARY

Army Form C. 2118

Instructions regarding War Diaries and Intelligence Summaries are contained in F.S. Regs., Part II. and the Staff Manual respectively. Title Pages will be prepared in manuscript.

(Erase heading not required.)

Place	Date	Hour	Summary of Events and Information	Remarks and references to Appendices
RANCOURT	12.1.17		Fairly Heavy shelling all day but at 5.15 PM a strong barrage opened a whole hour for 15 minute, nothing however noticed and ceased at 5.30 PM. 121st Brigade relieved 120th in RANCOURT SECTOR, 120th BRIGADE becoming Divisional Reserve, Relief started at 6 P.M. completion. Batt. relieving 20th Middx: relief at 9.50 PM halt, proceeded from MAUREPAS by motor lorries at 9.50 PM.	
CAMP.	13.1.17		CAPT 17. CAPT. BINGHAM. M.O went down sick. Draft of 28 O.R. received.	
	14.1.17 to 15.1.17		All men resting. Draft of 64 O.R. received. Temp. M.O reports Lt. R.C. HEWITT from 136. FIELD AMB. Men refitting and doing lightwork, physical drill etc. All men of Battalion with new hard foot powder, which almost the win and men are all men feet impulse are in fairly good condition.	
	15.1.17		120th Brigade relieved 119th Brigade in NORTH BOUCHAVESNES SECTOR. Batt. left Camp 17 at 11.0 % relieving 18th WELSH as in brigade support at ASQUITH FLATS. Relief complete 1.40 P.M. ACCOMODATION Very cramped as two halt occupy what was originally	

1875. W. W595/826. 1,000,000. 4/15. J.B.C. & A. A.D.S.S./Forms/C. 2118.

WAR DIARY or INTELLIGENCE SUMMARY

Army Form C. 2118

Place	Date	Hour	Summary of Events and Information	Remarks and references to Appendices
ASQUITH FLATS	19.1.17 to 22.1.17		Health very well. Are great covered by 1-2" Snow. ALL MEN employed in cleaning dug outs and generally improving condition. All men's feet afair doubts with new Trench foot powder. Had Reft ASQUITH FLATS at 4.30 PM to relieve 13th E. SURREYS in Left Subsection N. BOUCHAVESNES. AGILE TRENCH now very good as thereway to B.H.Q. No men not on duty are shaving. Relief completed at 10 P.C.P.M.	
NORTH BOUCHAVESNES	23.1.17		Hazy day no improved our accommodation for H.Q. personnel very scarcity. Coy's upon than not much work done on par of men on part how. Quiet night much clearer of artly. Quiet day. C.O. returns of leave. Weather very cold. 200 pmn during night. unusual intermittent shelling.	
	24.1.17		Quiet day. Unusual intermittent shelling. G.O.C. 8th Div visited H.Q. looking in line preparation relieving Div. Felt by relief.	
	25.1.17		Much aerial activity between very quiet day, still very cold. C.O. 1st NOTTS & DERBYS (24th BRIG) VISITED HQ. to arrange detail for relief.	

WAR DIARY
INTELLIGENCE SUMMARY
(Erase heading not required.)

Army Form C. 2118

Place	Date	Hour	Summary of Events and Information	Remarks and references to Appendices
NORTH BOUZAVESNES (CAMP 124)	26.1.17		24th Inf Brigade relieved 10th Inf Brigade. Batt. relieved by 1st NOTTS & DERBY'S relief of ration at 5 P.M. completed 5.30 P.M. Proceeded to MAUREPAS. Thence by motor lorries to Camp 124. (SAILLY LAURETTE)	
CORBIE	27.1.17 to 29.1.17		Left Camp 124 at 11.30 AM and proceeded by motor lorries to Corbie to CORBIE. Officers & men in billets, fairly good on the whole but cold owing to lack of fuel. D.I. became Corps reserve. 2nd Lieut. G.G. MACPHEE (D) JOINED for duty & 22nd Jan. and posted " R.B. BONSOR (D) to Coys as shewn. " J.G.B. WALKER (c) " D.M. CAMERON (B)	
	30.1.17 to 31.1.17		Spent cleaning up and refitting with light work in morning. 2nd Lt. Warren D.R. gone on ride Capt. BALLANTYNE taken over Adjutant temporarily. Coys employed in reorganising platoons, physical drills etc in the afternoon recreation.	

WAR DIARY
or
INTELLIGENCE SUMMARY

Place	Date	Hour	Summary of Events and Information	Remarks and references to Appendices
CORBIE	31.1.17		Extract from London Gazette. Jan 16th 1917. Temp 2nd Lieuts to be Temp Lieuts. T.K. Chalmers (July 1st 1916) A.B. Burton (Oct. 24th 1916) Lieut A.B. Burton is appointed Temp Capt whilst in command of A Coy. will effect from 17-12-16 Total casualties for month. 5. O.R. Killed. 5. O.R. Wounded.	

1st Highland I.

WAR DIARY or INTELLIGENCE SUMMARY

Army Form C. 2118

9 N
2 sheet

Place	Date	Hour	Summary of Events and Information	Remarks and references to Appendices
Caplie	1/2/17		2/Lt A. Watt to hospital from 40th Wit School Alloa on 30/1/17. Evacuated on 31/1/17. 2/Lt C.W. Strinsby went to hospital 31/1/17. Evacuated same day.	
	4/2/17		Relieve of Bde. by Brig. General Nicholson temporary command 120th Brigade. Captain B. Bingham wounded to England.	
	5/2/17		Lt. Col. P.M.A. Dick DSO took over command of 120th Brigade. Major H.P. Gores taking command of B." Received draft of 11 O.R.	
	7/2/17		2/Lt C. Ramsay went to hospital	
	8/2/17		Capt A.B. Burton — " —	
	9/2/17		3/Lt H. Fraser — " — 2/Lt P.B. Warren returned to duty 2/Lt J.W. Bruce joined for duty posted to A Coy	
	10/2/17		" E.J. Thompson went to hospital	
	12/2/17		" P.B. Warren took over duties of Adjutant from Capt Ballantine " J.C. Pratt went to hospital	
	14/2/17		At Caplie 14/ost Coy new being trained in fighting platoon formation + attack. Physical drill & bayonet fighting. Training of Specialist & recreation in the afternoon. Left Caplie 2.30 pm arrived Camb 112 at 4 pm.	
	15/2/17		Lt Hewitt went to hospital	
Camb 112	17/2/17		Captain G.C. Manford returned to duty took over duties of Adjutant.	
	18/2/17		Captain D. Nicholson went to hospital.	

WAR DIARY
or
INTELLIGENCE SUMMARY
(Erase heading not required.)

Army Form C. 2118

Place	Date	Hour	Summary of Events and Information	Remarks and references to Appendices
CAMP 11D	19/2/17		Captain F. B. McCarter reported for duty.	
	24/2/17		Captain A.B. Burton & 2/Lt E.J.T. Thompson returned to duty	
	27/2/17		Inspection of Company unit men held by A.D.M.S. & all is well.	
	12/2/17 23/2/17		Training of Military Lectures, Physical drill, Bayonet fighting. Men firing at range & throwing live bombs. Also undergoing fatigues, parties as required.	

TOTAL CASUALTIES FOR MONTH. NIL.

A. C——
14th H.L.I.

WAR DIARY
or
INTELLIGENCE SUMMARY
(Erase heading not required.)

Army Form C. 2118

Vol 10

10 N Eshuela

Place	Date	Hour	Summary of Events and Information	Remarks and references to Appendices
CAMP 112. BRAY.	1.3.17. to 6.3.17		Lt Col Dick D.S.O. returned from Commanding 120th Brigade and assumed Command of Batt. Batt. & Coy training in attack etc. 2nd Lieut Houston goes to Hospital from Alley. 2nd Lt. Thompson gor sick with Influenza. Lt Scott arrives and is posted to D. Coy. C.O. & Coy Commanders reconnoitre new line (SOUTH BOUCHAVESNES). 2nd Lieut Hutchinson reports and is posted to C Coy.	
Camp 19.	7.3.17		Batt. moves to Camp 19. SUZZANNE.	
HOWITZER WOOD.	8.3.17 to 9.3.17		Batt. moves to HOWITZER WOOD and relieves 2nd BATT A&S.H. (33rd Div.) and become Brigade reserve. 2nd Lieut Souran goes to base for dental treatment.	
BETHUNE ROAD.	10.3.17		Batt takes over right section (BETHUNE ROAD sector relieving 11th K.O.Y.L.I.	
"	11.3.17 to 12.3.17		Quiet day. Nothing of importance. Slight enemy shelling. no change reported.	
"	13.3.17		Batt relieved by 11th K.O.Y.L.I. with exception of Left Coy. Brigade hat now moved into 3 Sub sectors Left, centre & right. 14th H.L.I. remain Reliefs centre sub sector with remaining 3 Coys and Head quarter at. ROAD WOOD.	
"	14.3.17.		Quiet day, nothing of importance.	
"	15.3.17		Heavy enemy shelling in the north, a demand to move forward in Cayenlin with S4 div. a brigade Left by enemy vacate hat. Baker wounded in right eye. 9/15th/16th repair enemy still holding new line.	
"	16.3.17		2nd Lieut. 0/R12 Morrow to Barn on P.B. owing to his eyes 2nd " Smiles gone to Hospital 2nd " Pratt returns from hospital	

Army Form C. 2118

WAR DIARY
or
INTELLIGENCE SUMMARY
(Erase heading not required.)

Instructions regarding War Diaries and Intelligence Summaries are contained in F.S. Regs., Part II. and the Staff Manual respectively. Title Pages will be prepared in manuscript.

Place	Date	Hour	Summary of Events and Information	Remarks and references to Appendices
BETHUNE ROAD.	16.3.17		Quiet day. Further news of enemy retirement in the south. Major H.P. Coles left to proceed to England for a senior officers course. Patrols sent out during night (16/17) but enemy still holds our line.	
	17.3.17		Quiet day. Preparations for small raid a cross on BETHUNE ROAD on night of 16/17 during afternoon. Information received that 121st Brigade has occupied German front line. About 3 AM on night 17th/18th Batt occupied German front line. No enemy found. Brigade H.Q. moved forward to P.E. VIOLET. Batt H.Q.	
OLD GERMAN FRONT LINE.	18.3.17		Moved to crate in old German front line. C Coy pushed forward and occupied HAUT-ALLAINES. Remaining Coys consolidating new position and getting in touch with right and left. No sign of enemy.	
SUPPORT LINE.	19.3.17		Two Coys A+B under Capt. Ballantyne advance to aubain. 2 Coys 14th A.S.H. in left section line of resistance to BROUSSE TRENCH. Proceeded & got in touch with S.H. Div and Bdt. Brigade H.Q. outside Bin AIZECOURT le HAUT. MONT ST QUENTIN. Cyclist & yeomanry in touch with small patrols of enemy in DRIENCOURT + TEMPEAUX, LE FOSSE	
"	20.3.17		Major H.P. Coles returned from detail. Senior officers course postponed. 2nd Lieut RAMSEY returned from hospital.	
			WATT.	

WAR DIARY or INTELLIGENCE SUMMARY

Army Form C. 2118

Place	Date	Hour	Summary of Events and Information	Remarks and references to Appendices
VAUBAN Left section line of resistance 6th German reserve line	20.3.17		Major H.T. Coles took over command left section line of resistance from Capt. Ballantyne. Nothing to report.	
	21.3.17		Two Coys ordered to relieve 2 Coys 1st A&S.H on old outpost line. AIZECOURT La HAUT - MONT ST QUENTIN. 14th A&S.H now held outpost line TEMPEAUX-le-fosse - DRIENCOURT. Remaining two Coys 14th A&S.H with H.Q. established in AIZECOURT La HAUT. Lt Col Dick D.S.O. O.C. left section line of resistance from Bancourt 84th Div via AIZECOURT - La HAUT - BUSSU wood to MONT ST QUENTIN. 164th Brigade relieved by 119th Brigade. Rel. 14th H.L.I. 14th A&S.H. Relf 119th Bde.	
AIZECOURT LA HAUT.	22.3.17		Reconnoitred new defensive line TEMPEAUX-la-fosse - DRIENCOURT and fixed boundaries with right section, and allotted posts to Coys with portions of strong points. Batt working on new defensive line, repairing old German trench and moving in section of old defensive line, Italian dug-outs &c. 2/Lt Devens - 8th div to Capt Ballantyne's Coy down to detail. Lt Smith takes command of B Coy.	
	23.3.17 to 24.3.17			
HOWITZER WOOD	25.3.17		Batt relieved by a batty of the 143(?) brigade but owing to change of orders Batt not relieved but ordered to move out, last moved to Grandarin Hill wood. HQ H. Div. became Corps reserve.	

Place	Date	Hour	Summary of Events and Information	Remarks and references to Appendices
25.3.17 HOWITZER WOOD	25.3.17		Reinforcements. 114. O.R.	
	25.3.17		Rein/arrived. 43. O.R.	
			Capt Paton returned and posted to A. Coy in command	
			A/Capt Benton reverts to Lieut on ceasing to command A.Coy.	
			Capt Ferguson from leave posted to D Coy in command	
			Capt Sutern on return from leave from D Coy to B. Coy & takes over command	
			2nd Lieut. McKAY reported and is posted to D Coy.	
			Whole batt. on working parties new water main to Hill 150.	
	26.3.17		Strich all night. 2nd Lieuts. transferred to England 21.2.17	
	27.3.17		Capt. McKinnon " " 25.2.17	
			Capt. J. Nicholson " " 26.2.17	
	28.3.17 to 30.3.17		Battalion carrying on water main to Hill 150. Brigade staff ride.	
			6 spare officers.	
			Strength 9. 109. O.R. received 50 from Garr. & S.q. from Entrenching Battalion at ARRAS. new rather raw but will soon	
	31.3.17		Engineers in charge of water laying is found that is walk not on a mound, 10 Battalion R.E to undo all the work done. The OC C enquires which has been wanted.	

Army Form C. 2118

WAR DIARY
or
INTELLIGENCE SUMMARY
(Erase heading not required.)

Place	Date	Hour	Summary of Events and Information	Remarks and references to Appendices
HOWITZER WOOD	31.3.17.		To the casualties for month. 2. O.R. Killed. 7. O.R. Wounded.	

14th H.L.I.
31.3.17.

14 HL1 Army Form C. 2118.
Vol XI

11 N
2 sheets

WAR DIARY
or
INTELLIGENCE SUMMARY.
(Erase heading not required.)

Place	Date	Hour	Summary of Events and Information	Remarks and references to Appendices
HOWITZER WOOD	14.4.17 to 8.4.17		Taking up of life lines & training for attack	
QUINCONCE	24.17 to 22.4.17		Bn moved by Motor Lorries to Quinconce. A PÉRONNÉ & gave into camp thereon. Employed under R.E. for laying track for Decauville railway	
EQUANCOURT	22.4.17		Bn moved by Motor Bus to EQUANCOURT. into billets	
	23.4.17		C & D company commanders go on a recce of line. D & B Battalions employed in rebro DESERT WOOD & east there. 11.30 PM Batt moved to Rd of position as support to the 6 H.L.I. Enemy high explve shell on	
	24.4.17		KILLERS PLODISH. ZERO 4.15 AM Barrage commences. 4.17 AM German barrage commences 4.30 AM East Surrey Regt report German trench captured. Enemy high explve capture of VILLERS PLOUICH & call for reinforcements.	
		5.45 AM	B. Coy moved forward to cross roads R13 a.5.3	
		5.48 AM	C. Coy moved forward the village heavily	
		6.72 AM	Germans bombarded the village & our village limits commenced. Defensive plan formed on left. The night passed without incident.	

WAR DIARY or INTELLIGENCE SUMMARY

Place	Date	Hour	Summary of Events and Information	Remarks and references to Appendices
VILLERS PLOUICH	23.4.17		E. Surrey Regt & H.H.Y relieved by Yorks Regt under Lt Col Baker	
	26.4.17		recaptured. H.L.I. bivouacked in BOUZEAUCOURT WOOD. 1st H.H.Y. marched to billets in ETRICOURT. About 250 prisoners captured in VILLERS PLOUICH and several machine guns. Many souvenirs	
ETRICOURT	27.4.17 to 30.4.17		Casualties 2 officers 109 O.R. excluding 9 men killed	

J Nicholas Major
1st H.L.I.

WAR DIARY
INTELLIGENCE SUMMARY

(Erase heading not required.)

Army Form C. 2118.

14 HLI
8/5/17

Place	Date	Hour	Summary of Events and Information	Remarks and references to Appendices
Queens Cross	1.5.17		The Batt. was relieved by 10th I. Fus.@ Right sub sector 133rd Inf. Bde. on the front line at VILLERS PLOUICH.	
VILLERS PLOUICH	2.5.17 to 6.5.17		The Battalion was pushed forward. Their was no shell fire.	
QUEENS CROSS	6.5.17 to 12.5.17		The Batt. was relieved by 13th R. Surrey Regt. went into Rest billets at QUEENS CROSS. On the 12th the Batt. was relieved by the 11th R.S.L. 6.21st Regt. 20th Div. & spent the night 12/13. 26 HEUDICOURT. were we relieved the 10th Durham Cameliers 20th Bde. 8th Div. who came Divisional Reserve for the GONNELIEU SECTOR	
LINE	13.5.17 to 18.5.17		The Battalion went into the Sine Right Batt. entire Brigade. During the whi[ch] the enemy made a raid on our trenches although Officers NC.O.R this over and they stage was after a time. & charged into the enemy 2 N.C.R. returned enemy bombers were though our wire. Not many injured.	
	18.5.17		Batt. relieved by 1 Nr. 2 Hampshires that went into Bay Suffolks on Farm road.	12 N 2 members

WAR DIARY
or
INTELLIGENCE SUMMARY.
(Erase heading not required.)

Army Form C. 2118.

Place	Date	Hour	Summary of Events and Information	Remarks and references to Appendices
	25.5.17		Near Villers Bretch on Sunken Road – 2 O.R. killed, 4 O.R. wounded and 3 officers lightly wounded. Lieut. C. Lutus was evacuated. The infantry of addition being protected by a barrage of smoke gas, consolidated known within 5 long way from enemy.	
LINE	28.5.17 to 31.5.17		Batt. relieved by 114th Shines braubine (3rd Div) n. relieved the R. + L in front of LA BASQUERIE. Left Batt. Light Bngd. The line occupied by a series of posts pieced up by a shallow trench. The enemy very active on this front. No time fatherers (returning) was carried out but no enemy encountered.	
			Lieut M.A. Dobson to C.R.E. treats. Numer 21/5 Effective strength. May s/t officers 43 O.R. 803 " " " " 40 " 878	
			Casualties 1 Officer wounded O.R. Killed 5. Died of wounds 5. Wounded 29. Non 21 duty on self inflicted	1/H 1/H 1/H 1/H 1/H 1/H 1/H 1/H 1/H 1/H

14 HLI
Vol 13

18 IV
2 sheets

WAR DIARY
or
INTELLIGENCE SUMMARY.
(Erase heading not required.)

Army Form C. 2118.

Place	Date	Hour	Summary of Events and Information	Remarks and references to Appendices
CONNELIEU SECTOR	1/7		Lt. Col. D.H.A. Dick assumes command of the Brigade during the absence of the Brigadier at the Division Hqrs. f.H. Tactic assumes	
	2/7		Command of the Batt. Line very quiet — our patrols reconnoitred no man's land every night but no enemy met with. Enemy still our batteries persistently but did little damage. Trenches were much improved during our tour & a new front line dug	
	3/7		The Batt. was relieved by the 13 H.L. Lurry Regt & went into Support	
	4/7		The Batt. was in Support & provided working parties for the front line	
	6/7			
	10/7			
DESSART WOOD	11/7		The Batt. was relieved by the 21st Middlesex Regt & went into Reserve with the rest of the Brigade in DESSART WOOD	
	11/7		Time occupied in training during the morning — football etc in the	
	do		afternoon. Very hot — Camp moved out of wood of cooler system.	
	19/7		Platoon football competition produced excellent results game won by No 3 Platoon. Heavy thunderstorms	

Army Form C. 2118.

WAR DIARY
or
INTELLIGENCE SUMMARY.
(Erase heading not required.)

Instructions regarding War Diaries and Intelligence Summaries are contained in F. S. Regs., Part II. and the Staff Manual respectively. Title pages will be prepared in manuscript.

Place	Date	Hour	Summary of Events and Information	Remarks and references to Appendices
VILLERS PLOUICH	17/7		The Batt. relieved the 17th Welsh Regt on the left Sub. sector	
	19/6/17		VILLERS PLOUICH. Trenches full of water.	
			Line interesting – a good deal of sniping on both sides –	
	25/6		enemy sent over Light T.M.s otherwise quiet. Our patrols	
	28/6/17		reached "no-mans-land" but did not encounter the enemy.	
			Trenches defended & were much improved.	
FIFTEEN RAVINE	28/6/17		The Batt. was relieved by the 14th Batt. A.S.H. & went into support	
	6/6 30/6/17		in 15 Ravine	

STRENGTH

	O.R.		June 1st	
Casualties	16		31 Offs. 866 O.R.	
			June 30th	
			39 Offs - 902 O.R.	

Arrivals

				Departures
2/Lt HARDING, F.D.M	25.6.17		2/Lt CLARKE, N.M	Evac to England sick 2-6-17
SOUDON, S.	25.6.17			
WATT, T.S.	28.6.17		Lieut SCOTT, J.M.	Transferred R.F.C.
Lieut HENDERSON, H.Y.G.	27.6.17			

H Jackson Major
1/7/17

M 41

Headquarters
120th Bde.

Confidential

Herewith War Diary for July.

CW Balfour
Lieut Col
Comdg 14th HIGH L.I.

31.7.17.

1917 Volume VII

14 HLI

Oct 14

Army Form C. 2118.

WAR DIARY
or
INTELLIGENCE SUMMARY.
(Erase heading not required.)

Place	Date	Hour	Summary of Events and Information	Remarks and references to Appendices
FIFTEEN RAVINE	1/7/17		Lt Colonel C.H. BATTYE D.S.O. King's SHROPSHIRE LIGHT INFANTRY assumes command of the Battalion. 29.6.17	
	2/7/17		Batt. in support. Gave conference and carrying up to front line. Improvement of shelters in 15 Ravine.	
	6/7/17		Batt. relieved 10th A & S from the left sub-sector.	
VILLERS PLOUICH	5/7/17		40th Division Shrapnel Glove. M.R.H.Q. headquarters who first work 12th elt 14 qy on Shall I Butt hurr of sub on number of S.A.A. on Mallies cast fired on close to H.Q.	
	11/7/17		between of light draught horses in number 9.2 S.A.A. Holding Cart.	
	12/7/17		Raid on enemy trenches carried out by "C" Coy 30 O.R. number 2/Lt E.D. Whistler. Sine Bangalore Tam Dugatres to Guelbers 24 th hours offset on enemy were by R.E. Zero draws very heavy & hostile for long time to get into position. gap 26 ft. but blown an able to enable lith of the explosion. Garden hastily manned into trench but found it unoccupied. Enemy bar took	

1 H N
7 meter

WAR DIARY
or
INTELLIGENCE SUMMARY
(Erase heading not required.)

Army Form C. 2118.

Place	Date	Hour	Summary of Events and Information	Remarks and references to Appendices
VILLERS PLOUICH	10/7		at twelve midnight about of enemy Black & white balls night. Remainder of night moved down trench like telephone wires bombed but no one hurt. No identification were obtained. Party returned safely 2 O.R. slightly wounded. During the two moves in was done or information of trenches which were very narrow places where no one again but orphans in front line patrols. No Mans Land very quiet. Double patrols sent out Enemy sent up very frequent flares at night on front line and G.S. were riddled at intervals with light Tr M C. Shells.	
66 BEAUCOURT TRECAULT ROAD	18/7		Batt is relieved by W.R. N. Highers into Bay Reserve in the GOUZEAUCOURT-TRESCAULT ROAD & marches and is near Conference in turn so down to DESCART WOOD for two days for baths & aeroplay on 30 yds range	Casualties 2 O.R.

WAR DIARY or INTELLIGENCE SUMMARY

Army Form C. 2118.

(Erase heading not required.)

Instructions regarding War Diaries and Intelligence Summaries are contained in F. S. Regs., Part II. and the Staff Manual respectively. Title pages will be prepared in manuscript.

Place	Date	Hour	Summary of Events and Information	Remarks and references to Appendices
LOOZENCOURT TRESCAULT ROAD	13/7 to 20/7		Making further reconnaissances of right & front line. Killing of some movement nature noticed. Capturing made good sniping. Batt. relieved 13th Tank Surrey Regt on the night Sept. 20/21st	
VILLERS PLOUICH	21/7			
VILLERS PLOUICH	28/7		A Raiding party of 35 O.R. from "B" Coy under 2/Lt J.T. PARKER left our trenches at 11.30 P.M. When bangalore tube was left long were taken out & the men hung suspended in enemy wire — bombs tried when all (12 & 15) wire located on our left flank. 2/Lt PARKER at once gave the order to rush & two sections rushed forward & the enemy through showing marked. On over after throwing bombs several of our men became casualties we were unable to knock out hidden Bugh trenched & all the enemy which were brought in. 2/Lt PARKER & Pte OSWIRLD carrying in & was much difficulty from enemy wire. Enemy opened very small arms & light MG fire. Came above 1 officer &	Captain W.M.

WAR DIARY or INTELLIGENCE SUMMARY

(Erase heading not required.)

Army Form C. 2118.

Place	Date	Hour	Summary of Events and Information	Remarks and references to Appendices
VILLERS PLOUICH	28/7		ent. to O.R. wounded mostly slight. That three of Coy ere covered whilst posted on the Hans Harel were bombs at H.Q. BRUCE, B + 3 O.R. were wounded & slightly. The wounded were brought in + later returned to No Man's land, but could not be discovered on leave of enemy right front.	
	29/7		About 6 A.M. enemy sent over 12 T.M. gun bombs on our right front. The enfilading also seemed to open up + our Lewis gun O.P. although hit by M.G. by slight grenades have until offering to have continued the advance repulsed. To keep dun and now left the enemy or other troops if the fusilre. It is difficult to tell whether or not any of...	Coln Wm

A6945 Wt. W14421/M1160 350,000 12/16 D.D.& L. Forms/C./2118/14.

WAR DIARY
or
INTELLIGENCE SUMMARY

Army Form C. 2118.

Place	Date	Hour	Summary of Events and Information	Remarks and references to Appendices
MILLERS PLACE	27/7		Owing to our good work in the line on front line communication	
	27/7		trenches were well made. We worked hard in	
	28/7		the bombing up all the days. The enemy shelled our	
			trenches rather heavily & put 7 pbs into the crater of	
			several times but little damage was done	
	28/7		Enemy fairly quiet, unknown windfall to reach our trenches	
			on right of left of left of left Coy front time during the night had was	
			shore off by shrapnel fire latest intelligence report was	
			that no Germans who had been there have been seen	
	29/7		Bath. in relieved by 14th H.L.I. & proceeded by tent in	
			15 Ravine	
PICTEEN	30/7		Two battalions H.Q. 15 Ravine on company Railway	
RAVINE	31/7		EMBANKMENT one Coy FOREAUCOURT - TRESCAULT ROAD	

WAR DIARY
or
INTELLIGENCE SUMMARY.
(Erase heading not required.)

Army Form C. 2118.

Place	Date	Hour	Summary of Events and Information	Remarks and references to Appendices
	July 2/17		Reinforcements	
			2/Lt A HUNT 7.7.17 O.R 23 including 2 y	
			" J.A. STEWART 7.7.17 who had previously	
			" T.M. BLACK 7.7.17 served with the Bath.	
			" G.L. DICKSON 7.7.17	
			July 7th — 0 R	
			Effective strength 40 904	
			Ration strength 29 661	
			July 28th Effective strength 44 880	
			Ration strength 30 885	
	3.7.17		Lieut. J.B. Ruston + Lieut W.N Baines attached to 13th	
			East Surrey Regt to command companies	
	6.7.17		Major H.P. Calvo reported from Senior Officers Course	
	21.7.17		Major H.P. Calvo attached 11 Bath R.W.F. 2/Lt Cannon and	
			11 wounded during month 2/Lt Tuno S4 D R wounded	

WAR DIARY

INTELLIGENCE SUMMARY.

(Erase heading not required.)

Army Form C. 2118.

1917 14 HL Vol 15

15N Sched

Place	Date	Hour	Summary of Events and Information	Remarks and references to Appendices
15 RAMNE	1.8.17		Batt. in Support.	
BEAUCAMP	2.8.17		Batt. relieved 11th Royal Scots in Right Sub Sector BEAUCAMP Sector. Line did not had condition little short seemed to be in happier frame of mind at present. No curative no offensive operations were under taken as there was too much work to be done in widening trenches & putting down trench bombs.	
13 RAINE	8.8.17		Batt. relieved by the 11th A.V.H. & 11th Kings Own Brigade Front held by two Battalions instead of three. Extract from D.R.O. No 350 8.8.17 "The Cmdr in Chief has awarded the Military Medal to:- (a) No 25036 Sgt Hugh HOLLIS H.L.I. When with a raiding party on the night of 14th/15th July 1917 Sgt. HOLLIS set an excellent example by his bravery & disregard for danger. His efforts were greatly instrumental in the successful withdrawal of our party & in getting all the wounded back to our lines.	

WAR DIARY or INTELLIGENCE SUMMARY

Army Form C. 2118.

Place	Date	Hour	Summary of Events and Information	Remarks and references to Appendices
15 RAVINE S.8.7			(6) No 29294 Pt PATRICK O'SULLIVAN H.L.I. For gallantry & utter disregard of danger on the night of the 28/29th July 1917 when out with a raiding party at Chester Farm. Having been cut & engaged Pt O'SULLIVAN was conspicuous throughout. Afterwards he remained out under heavy fire helping in the wounded.	
	9.8.17		Extract from D.R.O. 351. 9.8.17. The Corps General wishes to express his appreciation of the following act of courage on the part of No 29259 Pt JOHN BRYAN H.L.I. attached Div Employment Co. On Aug 2nd 1917 Pt BRYAN was on duty on traffic control near Cavany Farm & horses drawing a lvs limbered cart came towards his post. With great promptness & considerable risk Pt BRYAN rushed the reins & managed to bring the horses to a standstill after being dragged a distance of 130 yds. There were no bits in the animals mouths.	J.H. Oliver Major

WAR DIARY
or
INTELLIGENCE SUMMARY

Army Form C. 2118.

(Erase heading not required.)

Place	Date	Hour	Summary of Events and Information	Remarks and references to Appendices
IS RAIME	10.8.17		Extract from D.R.O No 352 10.8.17 The following Belgian decoration for gallantry in the field has been awarded Officier de l'Ordre de Leopold Lieut-Colonel D H A DICK D.S.O. On the 23rd April 1917 during an attack on the enemy position Lt Col Dick was in command of the support Battalion which he handled most skilfully. As senior officer in the village he rallied troops who were thrown into confusion & continued the advance. Batt relieved the 11th H.W the night and relief Beaucamp — KILLERS PLOUCH sector town holding of aeroplanes occurred not continued on Kieche	J M Hughes Major

Army Form C. 2118.

WAR DIARY
INTELLIGENCE SUMMARY.
(Erase heading not required.)

Place	Date	Hour	Summary of Events and Information	Remarks and references to Appendices
PILLERS	15/8/17		Extract from D.R.O No 355 15.8.17	
PLOICH			The Field Marshal Commander in Chief has awarded the Military Cross to :—	
			T/2nd Lieut IRVINE THEODORE PARKER HLI	
			For conspicuous gallantry on the night of the 20/21st July 1917 when in command of a raiding party. Being hotly engaged having reached the enemy wire a German party was seen on the flank. 2/Lt PARKER immediately rushed him to the attack & drove off the enemy by his skirmish whilst & enabled all our wounded were withdrawn to our lines	
Oar ZZAA Cocerant 17			Batt relieved by 4.L.I.H and Adrian L. Reaoie 2 Coys	
WooD			DESSART WOOD HQ & 2 Coys GUEZEMCOURT WOOD Journey was carried out under by arrangements	
	21/8/17		Batt. Relieved the A.L.H. in the night Gul under BEAOCAMP —	all Sept/05
			FILLERS PLOICH Relief	Mops

WAR DIARY
INTELLIGENCE SUMMARY
(Erase heading not required.)

Army Form C. 2118.

Place	Date	Hour	Summary of Events and Information	Remarks and references to Appendices
VILLERS PLOUICH	26.8.17 to 21.8.17		It was decided to hold the line by posts. Work was done on this posts - during nights in hand & made a generally improving them so as to withstand the weather, weaker numbers better, materials in front & support lines. Enemy very quiet. Casualties during the month. 3 O.R. killed, 19 O.R. wounded 1 O.R. missing. 0 O.R. Effective strength 48 - 847 Ration Strength 24 - 683 41 - 889 27 - 644	
	Aug 4th		Arrivals "O" 2/Lt H.H. LOUDON 25.8.17 2/Lt R.B. BONSOR to O.R.(over) 16.8.17 2/Lt C.C. JENNINGS to O.R.(over) 23.8.17	
	25th		Departures	
			Reinforcements received during month 14 O.R. mostly our own men	

			16 V 5 sheets

WAR DIARY or **INTELLIGENCE SUMMARY**
Army Form C. 2118.

September 1917 VOL. XVI

Place	Date	Hour	Summary of Events and Information	Remarks and references to Appendices
15 Ravine	1		On suffered training parties under R.E.	A.4.52.c N.E, S.E. BEAUCAMP 1:10,000
	6		The Batt'n returned to the MARSH on right. Lieut. Littler KILLERS & Pro'ch	
	10		A raiding party of 40 O.R. from A Coy with 1 Lewis gun and 2 Bangalores under 2/Lt A. Wath, entered an attempt to enter the enemy trenches at R.89.1.8 on the night of the 10/11th. The Bangalores were never known on the wire except No Man's Land. Considerably delayed the advance. Eventually the Bangalores were placed together & exploded in the enemy wire. The party entered but were held up by a second belt of high wire. 2/Lt Wath & 8 O.R got over the second belt of difficulty & entered the enemy trench. The enemy were unable to get over this wire. 2/Lt Wath & this six men went about 25 yds up the trench. There were never seen to a few bombs thrown by them wounding 2 men. The party opened rapid fire & rifle bombs. Lieut. Wath was known to be the only 3/Lt shot	

September 1917

WAR DIARY or INTELLIGENCE SUMMARY.

Army Form C. 2118.

VOL. XVI

Place	Date	Hour	Summary of Events and Information	Remarks and references to Appendices
VILLERS PLOUICH	11		At 6.30 p.m. 2 officers & 30 O.R. left our trenches to reconnoitre the gap in the enemy wire the previous night. Capt CARMICHAEL went forward with 4 men & found that the gap had been repaired with a knife-rest. He cut half through this with wire cutters but finding the gap was not sufficiently wide & that there was rapid fire from the trench, Capt CARMICHAEL retired rapidly. Fire from the trench & Capt CARMICHAEL returned rapid fire the enemy then threw some bombs wounding Capt CARMICHAEL & 1 O.R. slightly the party then withdrew.	
HAPPENCOURT WOOD	13		The Batt was relieved by the M.K.R. & H. & went into Reserve at LOUZEAUCOURT HOG5 & DESSART WOOD. Training was carried out under by arrangements met of having a day on the 30 yds range.	
VILLERS PLOUICH	19		The Batt relieved the M.K.R. & H. the enemy artillery were found to be more active than usual.	

III   September 1917   VOL. XVI

WAR DIARY
INTELLIGENCE SUMMARY

Army Form C. 2118.

Place	Date	Hour	Summary of Events and Information	Remarks and references to Appendices
VILLERS PLOUICH	22		A successful raid was carried out on the enemy trenches on the night of the 22/23rd by D Coy under Capt. Ferguson. Three gaps were cut by the Bangalore during the afternoon - one at the point of entry R.8a.S.L. & two junk gaps R.8a.2.7 and R.1d.2.15. The party went over in three waves in file. The first wave was closely followed by the others up. The first objective was (farm trench) the second objective was C.T. at R.8d.6.o.05. Zero hour was at 7.10 P.M. At Zero-5 another barrage was put down on HIGHLAND RIDGE by the Special Coy R.E. & in a few minutes completely blotted out PINE COPSE & COUILLET WOOD from view. At ZERO-4 the smoke from candles & P bombs swift in a dense cloud across No Mans Land. All three waves reached the first objective without being fired on. As the first wave were under 2ft HEDGE across FARM TRENCH, verey lights were seen running down to the left there	Ref 576° N.E.S.E. BEAUCAMP 1:10,000

WAR DIARY or INTELLIGENCE SUMMARY

Army Form C. 2118.

IV September 1917 **VOL XVI**

Place	Date	Hour	Summary of Events and Information	Remarks and references to Appendices
VILLERS PLOICH	22		took up a position issued with rifles & L.G. fire up the field Op. 57C	
			The fire checked the third wave in its advance down	N.E, S.E
			FARM TRENCH & when the Maton commander 2/Lt T.S. BEAUCAMP	
			WATT was killed the platoon took up a position along the hedge	1:10,000
			The first wave closely followed by the others went	
			straight on to the O, its objective Which the C.T. west of	
			the trench was ouled the mopping up completed their	
			task. Time dug outs were completely destroyed & another	
			containing 4 unwounded prisoners was captured. The only wounded	
			about 7 S.C. P.O. with 4 wounded & 6 unwounded prisoners	
			12 Germans were left dead on the number road about	
			the same number in FARM TRENCH & considerable numbers	
			(about 40) according to statements of prisoners were on the	
			dug outs which were destroyed. Our casualties were	
			2 Officers killed, 1 Officer slightly wounded, 2 O.R. killed	
			11 O.R. wounded	

WAR DIARY or INTELLIGENCE SUMMARY

Army Form C. 2118.

September 1917 Vol. XVI

Place	Date	Hour	Summary of Events and Information	Remarks and references to Appendices
15 RAVINE	25		The Batt. was relieved by the 14th H.L.I & went into Support in 15 Ravine	
	27		Lt Col BATTYE D.S.O assumes temporary command of the Brigade. & MAJOR J.H FOSTER takes over command of the Batt.	
			Casualties O.R	
			Killed O 1.9.17 Officers Strength 0 0	
			Wounded 4 Other ranks Strength 40 859	
			Died of wounds 1 26 634	
			Accidentally wounded 2 30 29.9.17 Officers Strength 38 1059	
			Arrivals 2/Lt J BEKERIDGE a.c. Other ranks Strength 27 869	
			" J. NAIRN Departures	
			" R. STEVEN Capt R.D BALLANTYNE 6th March 2767	
			2/Lt - J SOUTER 11917	
			2/Lt J.N STEWART K.R.F.C. 192	
			Reinforcements 287 O.R. J.H.Foster Major	
			10th H.L.I.	

WAR DIARY
or
INTELLIGENCE SUMMARY.
Army Form C. 2118.

1917 1/4th Bn. H.L.I.

Vol 17

Place	Date	Hour	Summary of Events and Information	Remarks and references to Appendices
VILLERS PLOUICH	1.10.17		The Batt. relieved the A&S.H. in the Right sub-sector. Extract from D.R.O. dated 30.9.17. The C.in.C. Commander has awarded the Military Medal to the following:— No 18956 Cpl D. MASTERTON During a daylight raid on the 22nd Sept 1917 when in charge of a Demolition party he, his men right up to the final objective with great dash & exploded a dug-out full of S.A.A. Afterwards with great coolness he carried two more dug-outs to be destroyed. No 28803 Sgt A. DOODY By his good leadership & excellent example during a raid on the enemy trenches on 22nd Sept 1917 this N.C.O. prevented the enemy from taking the Mopping Up party in the flank. He conducted the withdrawal of his party with great coolness & without casualties.	17N 5 mats

WAR DIARY or INTELLIGENCE SUMMARY

Army Form C. 2118.

1917 October

Place	Date	Hour	Summary of Events and Information	Remarks and references to Appendices
VILLERS PLOUICH			No 23826 Cpl M. WOOD When in charge of a Lewis Gun during a daylight raid on 22nd Sept. 1917 this N.C.O. successfully brought it into action & silenced a hostile machine gun which was enfilading our final objective. His steadiness & good judgement were of great assistance to the raiding party.	
			No 42694 L/Cpl C. E. COOPER As one of a Mopping up party during a daylight raid on 22nd Sept 1917 this N.C.O. displayed great courage & dash. The first to reach the enemy dug-outs he located an officer who attacked him & disposed of him & more invalids. He carried to capture several prisoners & in the complete destruction of the dug-outs.	

WAR DIARY
or
INTELLIGENCE SUMMARY.
(Erase heading not required.)

Army Form C. 2118.

1917

Place	Date	Hour	Summary of Events and Information	Remarks and references to Appendices
VILLERS PLOUICH			No 28904 Cpl J HARDMAN when in charge of the stretcher bearers during a daylight raid on 22nd Sept 1917. Cpl HARDMAN displayed great fearlessness & skill in collecting & evacuating the wounded under heavy fire. Extract from D.R.O. dated 8.10.17. The Military Cross is awarded to :- T/Lieutenant A.C. SMITH Highland Light Infantry. For gallant conduct and good leadership in a daylight raid on the enemy's trenches on 22nd Sept 1917. Under his direction nine dug-outs were cleared of the enemy & systematically destroyed. All garrisons who refused to come out were exterminated. so effect his success were sent back under escort. It was due to Lieut SMITH's example that the raid was so successfully accomplished & all the wounded brought back to our lines.	

October 1917

WAR DIARY or INTELLIGENCE SUMMARY.

Army Form C. 2118.

Place	Date	Hour	Summary of Events and Information	Remarks and references to Appendices
VILLERS PLOUICH	4.10.17		At 7 P.M. the enemy attempted to raid our trenches after a heavy bombardment on our front & support lines. Under cover of darkness he succeeded in getting to our wire but was driven off by rifle & Lewis gun fire having one wounded prisoner in our hands.	
	5.10.17		The Batt. was relieved by the 1st Oxford & Bucks Light Infantry & withdrew to RAILTON	
	6.10.17		The Batt. moved by Decauville Railway to PERONNE	
	8.10.17		The baths were inspected by the G. in C. Commander with thanks also for the good work we had done.	
BERNEVILLE	9.10.17		The Batt. moved by train to BERNEVILLE	
	28.10.17 to 9.10.17		Training – Lectures, Platoon & Coy. Battalion exercises were carried out, special attention being directed to the training of getting platoons into formation.	
	29.10.17		The Batt. moved by march route to POMMERA	

WAR DIARY or INTELLIGENCE SUMMARY

Army Form C. 2118.

October 1917

Place	Date	Hour	Summary of Events and Information	Remarks and references to Appendices
	1.10.17		Effective strength O O.R. 36 1069 Ration strength 27 870	
	30.10.17		Effective strength 42 992 31 873	

			Casualties O O.R.
			     Killed — 6
			     Died of W. — 1 Arrivals
			     Wounded — 7 Capt H.W.J. HUMMERY 14.10.17
			     Departures 2/Lt H. HILTON
			                                   A.R. SLANDERS 5.10.17
			 2/Lt C. RAMSEY G.D.K. att 16.10.17 D. THOMSON
			 Lt H.H. LOUDEN A.R.F.C. 22.10.17 W.B. MacGEORGE M.C.
			                                           F.G. McLEOD 13.10.17
			                                           H.M. THOMAS 13.10.17
			                                           F.G. WARD 26.10.17	

WAR DIARY VOLUME XVIII

Army Form C. 2118.

INTELLIGENCE SUMMARY.
(Erase heading not required.)

Place	Date	Hour	Summary of Events and Information	Remarks and references to Appendices
POMERA	1-11-17		Battn remained here until 16th Nov.	
"	14-11-17		Brigade Scheme — at which C in C was present — he reviewed himself — 20 very fine placed with product of operation — A few details were remarked on by the Div Commander.	
"	11-11-17		At en Battle mounted ground of Battn — Returned from Brigade.	
BERNEVILLE	16-11-17		Battn moved to BERNEVILLE	
COURCELLES	17-11-17		" " " COURCELLES-LE-COMTE	
BEAULENCOURT	19-11-17		" " " BEAULENCOURT — For all reinforcements kits dumped. Actual position of operation —also given at a Battn on an hours notice. — All details left behind.	
LEBUCQUIERES	21-11-17		Conference on 18-11-17. — All details left behind. Battn moved to LEBUCQUIERES — No camp — tents pitched at dark.	
HINDENBURG	23-11-17		2pm moved to HINDENBURG SUPPORT line o relieved 2/4 York & Lancs Battn became Div Reserve @ 119.d.d.81.b.	
SUPPORT			18th Inf Brigade —	
LINE			Brigade who were holding Bourlon Wood. Transport to HERMIES. 7.30pm Battn ordered up to support 121st Bde but sent back not required from Ney Wood — all under 1 hour notice.	

18 N Inhab

Army Form C. 2118.

WAR DIARY VOLUME XVIII

INTELLIGENCE SUMMARY.

(Erase heading not required.)

Place	Date	Hour	Summary of Events and Information	Remarks and references to Appendices
HINDENBURG SUPPORT LINE	22.11.17	9.30 a.m.	Battn moved to GRAINCOURT under orders 186. Bde - Ordered to take BOURLON VILLAGE along with 186. SUFFOLKS. Zero hour name afternoon. ZERO hour	
		3 p.m.	Moved to BOURLON WOOD thro barrage on GRAINCOURT and on to ANNEUX CHAPEL. Casualties fev - one platoon knocked out - before	
		12.30 p.m.	Tried to get into artillery formation - Received rendezvous 12.30 p.m. No definite	
		3.30 p.m.	Ordered to move for fight. At 2.30 moved - Entered village about 3.30 occupied with 3 Coys H. Stokes - former on hook N of BOURLON VILLAGE. One Coy lost direction - & eventually turned up & held in Reserve Rations	
BOURLON VILLAGE	23.11.17	12.30 a.m.	S.O.S. was brought up during night - Repeated message to Bde - It was thought that Bn. was off - H.Q. in BOURLON VILLAGE	
		6.30 a.m.	Sharp attack by enemy & a few casualties	
		7.15 a.m.	Lieut Col. C.W. Battye D.S.O. killed by M.G. fire.	
		8.15 a.m.	Major T.N. Tober wounded - but remained with Bn. until 4.30 pm.	
		8.45 a.m.	Attack beaten off -	
			Trench lost with 3 front Coys - Enemy in force in village	
		4.30 p.m.	Capt G.C. MANFORD ADJUTANT assumed Command of Battn.	

WAR DIARY
INTELLIGENCE SUMMARY.
(Erase heading not required.)

Army Form C. 2118.

VOLUME XVIII

Instructions regarding War Diaries and Intelligence Summaries are contained in F. S. Regs., Part II. and the Staff Manual respectively. Title pages will be prepared in manuscript.

Place	Date	Hour	Summary of Events and Information	Remarks and references to Appendices
BOURLON VILLAGE	25-11-17		Repeated attempts to reach 3 Coys beaten off by hostile M.G. fire in Bourlon Village.	
	25-11-17	4 A.M.	13th East Surreys arrived to mop up Village. — 3 Coys Centre Bn — 1 in Reserve. Later 1 withdrawn to beat off attacks. E.S. H.Q. established with us.	
		11.30 A.M.	Lt.Col. Ad. Warden E.S. acted to command all troops in Bourlon Area	
	26-11-17	4.30 p.m.	Evacuated Bn H.Q. from Village to Dugout. — Sgn. Job in Rear — Support to have been relieved by 169 Bde. — No touch with 3 front Coys.	
	27-11-17		Whilst attempting Evacuation thro' Bourlon Wood to HINDENBURG SUPPORT LINE again & picked up Stragglers. — 3 Coys still missing	
			Transport moved to BAPAUME	
	28-11-17		Moved from HINDENBURG LINE to BLAIREVILLE by march route & motor bus.	
	30-11-17		BLAIREVILLE refitting	

WAR DIARY VOLUME XVIII

INTELLIGENCE SUMMARY

Army Form C. 2118.

Place	Date	Hour	Summary of Events and Information	Remarks and references to Appendices
	1-11-17		Effective Strength. Off. 42 — O.R. 992	
			Rahin	
			— 31 843	
	30-11-17		Effective — 25 541	
			Rahin 16 445	
			DRAFTS 78 O.R.	
			Casualties Off. O.R.	
			17 426	
			Above includes killed, wounded & missing — Details below as known.	
			Killed :— Lieut Col C.W. Battye DSO (M.F.his)	
			Wounded :— Major J.H. Foster (M.G. his)	
			2/Lt. F.M. Black (M.G. his)	
			Missing :— Capt. W.A.C. Stevens, Capt. E.C. Smith, Lieut Haddock R 2/Lt.	
			A. Watt, 2/Lt. B.J.B. Maddoe, 2/Lt. Jordan S, 2/Lt. J. Beveridge, 2/Lt. H.	
			Hilton, 2/Lt. R.R. Glanding, 2/Lt. G. Thomson, 2/Lt. W.B. McGeorge, 2/Lt. H.M.	
			2/Lt. H.M.M. Thomas, 2/Lt. R.R. Hand, 2/Lt. J.G. McLeod.	
			Arrivals	
			Capt. H.E.C. Mackay. — 27-11-17	
			present Officer Commanding.	
			2/Lt. L.W. Gillart. 4-11-17	

DECEMBER 1917
VOLUME XIX
/14th H.L.I

Vol 19

19 N
5 sheets

WAR DIARY
INTELLIGENCE SUMMARY
(Erase heading not required.)

Army Form C. 2118.

Place	Date	Hour	Summary of Events and Information	Remarks and references to Appendices
BLAIRVILLE	1.12.17		Battn. remained here, fitting out with equipment to until 3.12.17	
ERVILLERS	3.12.17		Battn. moved to BELFAST CAMP ERVILLERS, Brigade being in Reserve with H.Q. at HAMELINCOURT. Battn. commanders and company commanders reconnoitred Left Brigade sector of Divisional front. Batt O.R arrive	
"	4.12.17		Bn. Commanders & Coy commanders reconnoitred Right Brigade sector.	
			Arrival of Brigade H.Q. at HAMELINCOURT 3hrs	
			Conference at Brigade & Bombing carried on	
"	5.12.17		Training in musketry, Lewis Guns & Bombing carried on	
"	6.12.17		LT.COL. J.F.N. BAXENDALE 1/1 HANTS CARABINEERS YEO. assumed command of the Battn	
"	10.12.17		Battn. remained at ERVILLERS - BELFAST CAMP - refitting & training until this date - working parties.	
CRUISELLES	10.12.17		Battn. moved into Brigade Reserve at CRUISELLES (less one coy (C coy) in close support to 14th A. & S.H. in JANET AVENUE). Companies to man posts and trenches in INTERMEDIATE LINE in event of S.O.S. signals, relieving the 13th YORKS therein.	
c CRUISELLES	14.12.17		Battn. remained as above all this date.	
HINDENBORG LINE	14.12.17		Battn. relieved 14th A & S.H. in RIGHT subsector of LEFT Brigade front. A, D, & B coys in front line. C coy & A coy 14th A & S H in close support.	
			Bn. H.Q. in LINCOLN SUPPORT	

DECEMBER 1917
VOLUME XIX
11th H.L.I

WAR DIARY
INTELLIGENCE SUMMARY
(Erase heading not required.)

Army Form C. 2118.

Place	Date	Hour	Summary of Events and Information	Remarks and references to Appendices
HINDENBURG LINE	15/12/17	3/pm	Attack by 119th Bde on our right.	
		6/pm	Projection of gas drums by Special Coy R.E. on our sector.	
"	16/12/17		Remained as above until this date.	
"	18/12/17		Battn relieved in right sub-sector of Left Brigade front by 13th YORKS	
ERVILLERS	18/12/17		Battn moved by ROUTE march to BELFAST CAMP, ERVILLERS.	
	19/12/17		2/i/c reconnoitred Corps Second line around ST LEGER WOOD	
"			C.O, 2/i/c, and coy commanders reconnoitred Corps 2nd line as above.	
"	22/12/17		Presentation of the MILITARY MEDAL to 11 O.R. by Corps Commander to:-	
			Nos 28806 Sgt Hallen T. 29233 Pte Moller W. 28896 Pte Sutherland T. 24192 Pte Webbie J. 23705 Cpl Stanley B.	
			42659 Pte Brown J. 12319 Pte Watson T. 29460 Pte Smith A. 28925 Pte McVey W. 201380 2/Cpl Eadie J.	
			28792 Cpl Sherwood J. (29576 Pte Roche T. wounded – in hospital – 8889 Pte Lewisham H awarded M.M)	
"	24/12/17		Battn reviewed at ERVILLERS until this date	
CROISELLES	24/12/17		Battn moved to CROISELLES and relieved 12th SUFFOLKS in Brigade Reserve.	
"	27/12/17		Remained as above until this date. Coy leave in Left support 6.14th A & S H	
ERVILLERS	27/12/17		Relieved as above by 15th ROYAL SCOTS – 34th DIV.	
ERVILLERS	27/12/17		Battn moved by Route march to BELFAST CAMP – ERVILLERS.	

Army Form C. 2118.

WAR DIARY
— or —
INTELLIGENCE SUMMARY.
(Erase heading not required.)

DECEMBER 1917   VOLUME XIX

1/4th H.L.I.

Place	Date	Hour	Summary of Events and Information	Remarks and references to Appendices
ERVILLERS	27/12/17		Battn. remained here until this date.	
MOREUIL	28/12/17		Battn. relieved 2nd ROYAL SCOTS in RT. SUB-SECTOR of RT. BDE. of 40th DIVN. FRONT — night relief. A, B, D coys. in front line, one coy/part	
"	30/12/17		Battn stations above. Heavy shelling of left coy. in SHEFFIELD SUPPORT. Sgt. Smith wounded.	
"	31/12/17		Battn. still as above. 6 p.m. D & C coys. changed over	

WAR DIARY
or
INTELLIGENCE SUMMARY.

DECEMBER 1917 VOLUME XIX

144 H.L.I

HONOURS AND AWARDS

The General Officer commanding the 40th Division has been pleased to mention in Divisional Routine Orders the gallant conduct of the following O.R.S. for their

The MILITARY MEDAL has been awarded by His Majesty the KING for devotion to duty and conspicuous gallantry in the field during active operations against the enemy on 23rd 24th & 25th November 1917:—

Nº 28804 Sgt Holton T, 29233 Pte Mellor W, 28896 Pte Sutherland J, 24192 Pte Willie J, 23705 Cpl Stanley B, 42695 Pte Brown J, 22319 Pte Watson J, 29460 Pg Smith Q, 28925 Pte McVey W, 201380 L/Cpl. Eadie J, 28792 Pte Greenhead J, 29576 Pg Roche J, 2889 L/Cpl Mahre W, D.C.M 32029 Pte Leishman H 28881 Sgt Murphy W.

THE MILITARY CROSS. to G/Capt. Walker J.G.B, Lt. Dickson G.L., 2/Lt. Black J. McK., Lt. Thomson E.T., Q.M. Hon. Lieut Dicks J., a/Capt Burton A.B (attached to 13th E. Surrey) Capt. McCarter F.B (R.A.M.C.)

WAR DIARY
or
INTELLIGENCE SUMMARY.
(Erase heading not required.)

Army Form C. 2118.

DECEMBER 1917
VOLUME XIX
14th H.L.I.

Place	Date	Hour	Summary of Events and Information	Remarks and references to Appendices
			O/r. O.R.	
	30/11/17		Effective Strength 25 541	
			Ration — 16.445	
	31/12/17		Effective — 35.828	
			Ration — 27.621	
			Drafts during the month = 224 O.R.	
			Officers arriving :- 6/12/17 Lt Col Baguenale J.F.N 1/9 17 Lt Curle R.F.N 1/4 LTs. 12/77	
			Jennings C.C., Martin H., Stewart D.L., Bruce C, Curle A.C. 1/2 McLaren T, Young J.R	
			2LTs. 7/17 Beaton G.W. Ogden J.C Henderson W.J. Ferguson J. 3/17	
			Casualties :- 12/12/17 1 O.R. wounded (c)	
			15/12/17 1 " " (a)	
			16/12/17 3 " " (c)	
			17/12/17 4 " " (c)	
			31/12/17 1 " " (c)	
			2/Lt. J. Heim evacuated to England sick 18.12.17	
			Lt. E.J.T. Thomson – To England because he wishes as medical student	

H.G Mackay Capt
2/i/c/c 14
31/12/17

WAR DIARY or INTELLIGENCE SUMMARY

Army Form C. 2118.

JANUARY 1918
VOLUME XX
14th H.L.I.

Place	Date	Hour	Summary of Events and Information	Remarks and references to Appendices
NOREUIL	1/1/18		Battn. in front line - Rt. subsector.	Y/B 20
"	2/1/18		Battn. relieved by 14th A.&S.H. in Rt. sub-sector. B coy. went into RAILWAY RESERVE as support coy. to 13th E. Surreys in RAILWAY RESERVE	
NOREUIL	3/1/18		Battn. moved by route march - platoons at intervals - on relief to DEWSBURY TRENCH in Bde. Support (PONTEFRACT TRENCH, IGAREE CORNER Bn. HQ in Sunken road C.10.a.7.0	
"	4/1/18		Battn. in Bde. Support. Enemy much quieter. Rt. Battn. CENTRE BRIGADE. Flammenwerfer west	
"	5/1/18		Battn. in Bde. Support.	
"	6/1/18		Battn. in Bde. Support. A coy. relieved B coy. in support to 13th E. Surreys in RAILWAY RES. Battn. relieved 14th A.V.S.H. in Rt. subsector with four companies in front line, left coy. taking over from Rt. Battn. right coy. one coy. 14th A.V.S.H. in close support in RAILWAY RESERVE.	
"	7/1/18 - 9/1/18		Battn. in Rt. subsector as above	
"	10/1/18		Battn. relieved in Rt. subsector by 14th A.V.S.H. Battn. moved to MORY SOUTH CAMP in 7th Division Reserve. Major A.H. Seagrim joined the Battalion for duty as second in Command.	
"	11/1/18 - 14/1/18		Battn. remained at MORY in Brigade Reserve	
MORY	14/1/18		Battn. relieved 14th A.V.S.H. in Rt. subsector - Beaumville railway transport to Gds. H.Q.	20N 3 sheets

A6945 Wt. W11422/M1160 350,000 12/16 D.D.&L. Forms/C/2118/14.

WAR DIARY
or
INTELLIGENCE SUMMARY.
(Erase heading not required.)

Army Form C. 2118.

14TH H.L.I. JANUARY 1918 VOL. XX 14th H.L.I.

Place	Date	Hour	Summary of Events and Information	Remarks and references to Appendices
Rt Subsector	15/1/18 & 16/1/18		Battn. remained in Rt. SUBSECTOR. Trenches falling in badly owing to thaw after frost.	
"	18/1/18		Battn. relieved by 14th A. & S.H. Battn. moved into Brigade Support in DEWSBURY TRENCH, IGARBE CORNER and old Brigade Headquarters. Bt. Hq in C19a70.	
NOREUIL	19/1/18 – 22/1/18		Battn. remained in Brigade Support.	
"	19/1/18		Lt. Col. Campbell proceeded to England on leave. Major A.H. Seagrim assumed command of the Battn.	
"	24/1/18		DRAFT of 63 O.R. arrived.	
Rt Subsector	23/1/18		Battn. relieved 14th A. & S.H. in Rt. Subsector.	
"	23/1/18		2/Lt J.D. Edwards joined for duty.	
"	23/1/18 – 29/1/18		Battn. remained in Rt. Subsector. Battn. relieved 26/1/18 by 14th A.&S.H and proceeded to thence march to MORY South Campin Brigade Reserve at MORY S. CAMP	
MORY	29/1/18 – 30/1/18		Battn. remained in Brigade Reserve.	
Rt Subsector	30/1/18		Battn. left MORY by route march and relieved 14th A.&S.H. in Rt. subsector of Brigade front.	
"	31/1/18		Battn. in Rt. subsector of Left Brigade front.	
			31/1/18.	H.B. Maclean Capt. for Major 1/c 14th H.L.I.

14th H.L.I.

WAR DIARY
or
INTELLIGENCE SUMMARY.

(Erase heading not required.)

Army Form C. 2118.

JANUARY 1918 VOL. XX 14th H.L.I.

Place	Date	Hour	Summary of Events and Information	Remarks and references to Appendices
	31-12-17		Effective strength = Offrs. 35 . O.R. 828	
			Ration " = " 27 . 621	
	31-1-18		Effective strength = " 42 . 834	
			Ration " = " 27 . 632	
			Drafts during the month = 63 O.R.	
			Officers coming during the month :- Major A.H. Leagum 10/1/18	
			Lt W.F. Rayburgh 11/1/18, 2/Lt T.D. Edwards 23/1/18, 2/Lt R.G.H. Lea	
			28/1/18, 2/Lt J.S. Robertson 28/1/18, 2/Lt. K. Reid 28/1/18	
			Lt M.H. Gray 28/1/18.	
			Casualties :- Lt. R.F.N. Circle evacuated to England sick	
			O.R. 2 wounded 3.1.18; 1 wounded 5.1.18; 1 killed 7.1.18	
			2 wounded 7.1.18 ; 3 wounded 8.1.18 ; 1 killed 8.1.18	
			1 wounded 9.1.18 ; 1 wounded 19.1.18 ; 1 killed 16.1.18	
			2 wounded 23.1.18	
			Total 13 wounded 3 killed	
				Helmsley Capt. 31/1/18. for Major 14th H.L.I.

Army Form C. 2118.

WAR DIARY
or
INTELLIGENCE SUMMARY.

February 1918

Volume XXI
14th Somerset Light Infantry

(Erase heading not required.)

Instructions regarding War Diaries and Intelligence Summaries are contained in F.S. Regs., Part II. and the Staff Manual respectively. Title pages will be prepared in manuscript.

Place	Date	Hour	Summary of Events and Information	Remarks and references to Appendices
NOREUIL	1st Feb.		Battalion in front line right subsector	
"	3rd "		" relieved by 14th A.S.H. in right subsector & Brigade support One Coy in DENSBURY TRENCH – One at IGAREE CORNER & two in Sunken road. Batt. Bde. H.Q. C9a 9.5	
"			Batt. H.Q. at IGAREE CORNER. 1 O.R. killed	
"			In Brigade Support	
"	4th 5th 6th "		Batt. relieved 14th A.S.H. in front line right subsector	
"	7th "		" in front line	
"	8th 9th "		"	
"	10th "		" relieved in front line right subsector by 2/6 W. Batt. South Staffs Regt. Div new disposition of 7/6 O.Cliff. — 1 Coy Right Front 2 platoons in front line & 2 platoons in Support in RAILWAY RES. — 1 Coy Left Front with 2 platoons in front line & 2 platoons in support in COOKE ALLEY. 2 platoons of another Coy in RAILWAY RES. & 2 platoons in JEWSBURY — One Coy in JEWSBURY – BATT. H.Q. OC11C 6.9 1 O.R. wounded	
MORY			On relief Batt moved by march route to South Camp MORY for 1 night.	
BLAIRVILLE	11th "		Entrained in Leacanville for No 2 Camp BLAIRVILLE. Transport moved from Lysars Camp by road.	
"	11th/20th		At BLAIRVILLE Training. Div. in Corps reserve	

21 IV
2 sheets

J.M. Bayer---
Comdg 14th L.H.I.

Army Form C. 2118.

WAR DIARY
or
INTELLIGENCE SUMMARY.
(Erase heading not required.)

February 1918
Volume XXI
14th Highland Light Infantry

Place	Date	Hour	Summary of Events and Information	Remarks and references to Appendices
BLAIRVILLE	21st		Batt. moved by motor lorries to DURHAM LINES BOISLEUX-AU-MONT. Demonstration Platoon & 1 Sect. 224th Coy R.E. attached. Transport moved in rear of Batt.	
BOISLEUX- AU- MONT	22nd		Major Seagram to command 110th H.L.I.	
	23rd		Batt. Training – Musketry & Wiring practice	
			Supplied working party of 570 for digging a wiring new line in front of HENINEL	
	26th		" " " " " " " " WANCOURT	
			Major Hope D.S.O. reported and assumed in Command vice Major A.P. Seagram promoted and 19th Batt. H.L.I.	
	27th		Enemy up camps to prior to move to BASSEUX AREA	
			Batt. moved by motor lorries to POMMIER. Transport in rear of Batt. Div. in G.H.Q. reserve.	
POMMIER	28th			
			31-1-18 Effective strength 42 officers and 834 O.R.	
			Ration " 27 " " 632 "	
			28-2-18 Effective " 45 " " 753 "	
			Ration " 29 " " 724 "	
			Drafts during month:- 33 O.R. joined on 7/2/18 – 77 O.R. joined on 12/2/18 Total 110 O.R.	
			Officers reporting during month:- Capt. R.C. McCardie, Lt. J.R. Barclay C/o Lt. R. Hutchison on 12/2/18 from 17th H.L.I. Capt. A.J. Hope 21/2/18 from 17th H.L.I.	

J.M. Assendale Lt Col
Comdg 14 H.L.I.

40th Division.
120th Infantry Brigade

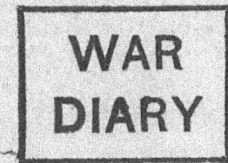

14th BATTALION

HIGHLAND LIGHT INFANTRY

MARCH 1 9 1 8

14TH HIGH. L.I.   120TH BDE. 40TH DIVN

WAR DIARY
or
INTELLIGENCE SUMMARY
(Erase heading not required.)

Army Form C. 2118.

22 N
8 sheets

Place	Date 1918	Hour	Summary of Events and Information	Remarks and references to Appendices
DURHAM CAMP BOISLEAUX	1/3/18		Battalion in DURHAM CAMP - BOISLEAUX. Battn. furnished working parties	
			on CORPS line at ST. MARTIN - SUR - COJEUL.	
"	2/3/18		do. do.	
POMMIERS	8/3/18		Battalion left DURHAM CAMP and moved by route march to POMMIER.	
	9/3/18		Battalion remained at rest at POMMIER.	
	10/3/18		Battalion practicing by platoons and companies, also as a battalion in Brigade	
	11/3/18		in attack.	
ERVILLERS	12/3/18		Battalion left POMMIER (6.30pm) and moved by route march to ENISKILLEN	
			CAMP - ERVILLERS.	
	13/3/18		Battalion remained at ENISKILLEN CAMP - ERVILLERS - exercising	
	to		in platoon and company work & attack practices by companies	
	20/3/18		Battalion furnished 500 strong working party cable burying at	
	18/3/18		(L'HOMME MORT (sheet 57 C.N.W B 17.a)	
	20/3/18		Battalion on working party as above. Standing at 1 am. 21/3/18	
	21/3/18	3am	Battalion stood to at 3am as heavy gun fire had broken out	
			along whole CORPS front.	
		5am	Enemy commenced shelling camp in ERVILLERS AREA	

14th H.L.I.

120TH Bde. 40TH DIVN

Page II

WAR DIARY or INTELLIGENCE SUMMARY.

MARCH, 1918.

Army Form C. 2118.

Place	Date	Hour	Summary of Events and Information	Remarks and references to Appendices
ERVILLERS	21/3/18	7 am	All map references are to SHEET 57 C.N.W. Battalion moved out of camp, and lay down in artillery formation in B.13.b. and B.14.a. awaiting orders. Shelling of area continues. Several casualties. (see appendices)	
MORY		3 pm	Battalion moved in artillery formation across country to position in the army line south east of MORY (B.29.a.b. and d.) A and C coys in the firing line, B and D in support. Support companies in B.28.b. and D. Batt. H.Q. at B.29.a.2.2. Battalion now in Brigade support to 10/11 H.L.I. and 14th A.+S.H.	
VAULX VRAUCOURT	22/3/18	1 am	Battalion moved by night in artillery formation to VRAUCOURT and VAULX-VRAUCOURT, and occupied positions to the NORTH of village. A coy in trenches in C.20.c. and C.19.d., C coy in posts in C.19.d., C.19.c. and B.24.b., B and D coys in support in C.25.b. & C.25.a. Batt. H.Q. in trench in C.19.c. Batt'n acting in Brigade Support to 14th A+S.H. and 10/11th H.L.I.	
do		7 am noon	Heavy shelling of area by enemy.	
do		1 pm	Enemy attacked in force positions in CORPS line held by 14th A.+S.H. + 10/11 H.L.I.	25/3/18

14th H.L.I.

WAR DIARY 120th Bde. 40th Div.n   Army Form C. 2118.
or
INTELLIGENCE SUMMARY.   MARCH, 1918.

Page III

(Erase heading not required.)

Place	Date	Hour	Summary of Events and Information	Remarks and references to Appendices
VAULX	22/3/18	2 pm	Large numbers of Germans are advancing in a south-westerly direction	
VRAUCOURT			over the slopes in C.21 and making for the valley of L'HIRONDELLE near VRAUCOURT on our right reported to have fallen back leaving	
			right flank of the division in the air.	
	do.	3 pm	Our Captain reports he began to move our their positions, moving south down the ECOUST - VRAUCOURT road.	
		4 pm	Battalion ordered to form a defensive flank along the VRAUCOURT - BEUGNATRE road facing east.	
			C. coy 14th H.L.I. and elements 9/14th A.I.F. continued the defensive flank by pushing up platoons to VRAUCOURT village. Enemy advance arrested for some time, but fresh columns of enemy infantry and Tanks were observed moving along ridges in C.21 to resume enemy attacking troops.	
ARMY LINE at		6 pm	Battalion withdrew to the ARMY LINE in B.29 a & c. C coy remained in the trenches of the ARMY LINE with elements	
MORY			of the 59th Division and the other battalions of the Brigade.	[signature]

14th H.L.I.
120TH BDE. 40TH DIVN.

Army Form C. 2118.

WAR DIARY
or
INTELLIGENCE SUMMARY.

Page IV   MARCH, 1918.

(Erase heading not required.)

Place	Date	Hour	Summary of Events and Information	Remarks and references to Appendices
ARMY LINE at MORY	22/3/18	7 p.m.	A, B and D companies remained in support behind the ridge in artillery formation.	
		9 p.m.	A, B and D companies moved into the ARMY LINE joining up with the 119th Brigade which held MORY. Batt. H.Q. at B.29.a.2.2.	
do	23/3/18		Enemy observed moving in trench along road from VRAUCOURT to MORY. All companies of the battalion engaged in heavy close quarter fighting in repelling constant enemy attacks to gain a footing in MORY village. ARMY LINE heavily shelled.	
do	do	10 p.m.	Rearrangement of companies in the army line, and withdrawal of elements of 52nd Division from the army line. C coy. on the right, D coy. 2 platoons in the ARMY line and 2 platoons in support in sunken road in B.29.a, A coy continuing to the left in the army line, and in 6 counterattack in B.28.b, and B coy continuing the line towards MORY.	
do	24/3/18		Battalion still in the ARMY LINE. Heavily shelled all day and subjected to incessant attacks by enemy between MORY and	

14TH H.L.I.

WAR DIARY 120TH BDE. 40TH DIVN Army Form C. 2118.

or

INTELLIGENCE SUMMARY.

Page V

Place	Date	Hour	Summary of Events and Information	Remarks and references to Appendices
ARMY LINE at MORY	24/3/18	7 pm	Enemy succeeded in breaking through the Division on our right, and threatened our right flank. A defensive flank was subsequently formed by the battalion and Coy of the 40th Battalion M.G.C. Enemy attack on night front of Battalion broken up by our Lewis gun fire	
do	do	10 pm	Orders received for all troops to evacuate positions held in the ARMY LINE and to occupy trenches in B.27 and H.2 thereby continuing our line from the division on the right to the Brigade on our left.	
BEHAGNIES	25/3/18	8.50 am	Battalion in position near BEHAGNIES. Enemy attacked heavily from direction of BEUGNATRE and FAVREUIL. Enemy advance and his enveloping movement around shoulder of position held up completely until 2 pm	
do	do	2 pm	14th A&S.H. who had the western end of the position withdrew	
do	do	4 pm	14th HLI 10/11 HLI and elements of the battalions still according to orders Lt Col Baynsdale wounded Capt H.G.S. Mackey assumed command	

14th H.L.I.

WAR DIARY 20TH BDE 40TH DIVN

INTELLIGENCE SUMMARY.

Page VI

Place	Date	Hour	Summary of Events and Information	Remarks and references to Appendices
BEHAGNIES	25/3/18	4 p.m.	Remained in position in the square of trenches to the east of Officers' Club at BEHAGNIES. Attempts by enemy to work round left flank ceased, but he began to make progress towards enveloping the position on the right, through the woods to be to the S.W. of the Club at BEHAGNIES.	
do	do	4.30 p.m.	The battalions of the other two brigades of the division seen retiring towards GOMIECOURT between BEHAGNIES and ERVILLERS. Position now being very heavily shelled.	
do	do	4.35 p.m.	Orders received by O.C. 14th H.L.I. to evacuate position at BEHAGNIES with all troops present to GOMIECOURT. Evacuation carried out under most intense machine gun fire by the enemy and heavy shelling.	
GOMIECOURT	do	5 p.m.	Elements of battalion + 10/11 H.L.I. occupied trenches in B 25 and A 30. Temporarily held enemy pursuit in check.	
do	do	7 p.m.	Battalion concentrated at GOMIECOURT and marched in artillery formation to AYETTE	

14th H.L.I.   120TH BDE. 40TH DIVN

WAR DIARY
or
INTELLIGENCE SUMMARY.

Army Form C. 2118.

Page VII

Place	Date	Hour	Summary of Events and Information	Remarks and references to Appendices
AYETTE	25/3/18	10 pm	Battalion rested in abandoned houses at AYETTE and DOUCHY Area	
ADINFER WOOD	26/3/18	9 am	Battalion moved by route march to ADINFER WOOD and took up a position astride the DOUCHY – MONCHY wood facing E.	
			14th H.L.I. on the right, 14th A.& S.H. on the left, and 10/11th H.L.I. in Brigade Support	
		3 pm	Brigade moved to left and occupied half the front of the 14th Brigade	
			A.& S.H. having been placed by intrbayer Batt of the 119 BDE	
ADINFER WOOD	27/3/18	1 am	Brigade withdrawn from position and moved by route march via ADINFER, RANSART, RIVIERE, BEAUMETZ, GOUY, FOSSEUX, BARLY, SOMBRIN to WARLUZEL 5 miles	
WARLUZEL	27/3/18	4 pm	Battn billetted at WARLUZEL	
do	28/3/18		Battn rested at WARLUZEL. Details under Major A.H. Seagrim joined the battalion. Major A.H. Seagrim took command of the Battalion	
WARLUZEL	29/3/18	7 am	Battalion moved by bus and route march to MONCHY-BRETON men who had been in the line by bus, others by route march	

[signature]

14th H.L.I.   120th Bde. 40th Div.

WAR DIARY
or
INTELLIGENCE SUMMARY.
(Erase heading not required.)

Army Form C. 2118.

Page VIII

Place	Date	Hour	Summary of Events and Information	Remarks and references to Appendices
MONCHY BRETON	29/3/18	5 pm	Battalion billeted at MONCHY-BRETON.	
do	30/3/18	10 am	Battalion moved by motor march to near DIEVAL and entrained and proceeded to NEUF BERQUIN where it detrained at 4 pm	
SAILLY-SUR-LA-LYS	30/3/18	5 pm	Battalion billeted at SAILLY SUR LA LYS	
SAILLY SUR LA LYS	31.3.18		Battalion remained at SAILLY SUR LA LYS	
do	do	8 pm	Battalion moved into front line at FLEURBAIX sector relieving 2/10th K.L.R. during the night 31st March / 1st April.	

Total Casualties 21/3 – 6/24/3 = OFFICERS – Killed 3. wounded 3. missing 1
O. RANKS – Killed 19. wounded 106. missing 124.

Total Effective Strength 26.2.18 = OFFICERS 47. OR 1009
" " " 28.2.18 = " 28 " OR. 482.
Total Effective Strength 31.3.18 = " 41 " 75 6
" " " 31.3.16 = " 28 " 641 5

[signature]
OFFICER REINFORCEMENTS = 2/Lt. NICOLSON, R.D.W.

Comdg. 14th H.L.I.

40th Division.
120th Infantry Brigade.

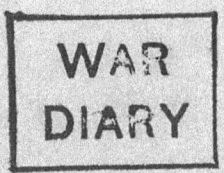

14th BATTALION

THE HIGHLAND LIGHT INFANTRY

APRIL 1918

14th HIGHLAND LIGHT INFANTRY • 120TH BDE • 40TH DIVISION

WAR DIARY or INTELLIGENCE SUMMARY
Army Form C. 2118.
VOL. XXIII
PAGE 1

Place	Date	Hour	Summary of Events and Information	Remarks and references to Appendices
FLEURBAIX 1918	night of 31/3/18 – 1/4/18		Battalion relieved 2/10th (Scottish) K.O. Liverpool Regt. in the right subsector of divisional front.	
"	1/4/18 – 5/4/18		Battalion in right subsector of divisional front.	
"	night of 6th/7th April		Battalion relieved in right subsector by 13th East Surrey Regt. and marched to billets at NOUVEAU MONDE.	
NOUVEAU MONDE	7th/8th April		Battalion in billets at NOUVEAU MONDE.	
"	9th April	4 A.M.	Bombardment of LE NOUVEAU MONDE commences.	
"		4.30 am	Order from Brigade to stand to.	
"		4.45 am	Warnng orders issued to Coy. Commanders for Battn. to move to its position in accordance with the Brigade standing defence scheme.	
"		5.15 am	Orders from Brigade to make up men to 170 rounds.	
"		6.15 am	Orders from Bde. to move to an assembly position about G.29.c.	
"		6.25 am	Battn. moves off.	
LAVENTIE		7.10 am	B.H.Q. takes up position at G.28.a.8.7	
"		8 am	Companies in their assembly position in G.29.c.	

14TH HIGHLAND LIGHT INFANTRY 120TH BDE. 40TH DIVISION
APRIL 1918.

Army Form C. 2118.

WAR DIARY
or
INTELLIGENCE SUMMARY.

VOL. XXIII PAGE II

(Erase heading not required.)

Instructions regarding War Diaries and Intelligence Summaries are contained in F. S. Regs., Part II. and the Staff Manual respectively. Title pages will be prepared in manuscript.

Place	Date	Hour	Summary of Events and Information	Remarks and references to Appendices
LAVENTIE	9th	9 A.M. (app.)	Orders from Brigade for Battalion to move forward into positions laid down to be occupied in Bde. defence scheme.	
"		10.6 am	All coys. have moved off from position of assembly to their forward positions which were as follows:- 3 coys. in the front line deployed in depth from LAVENTIE EAST POST (exclusive) to CHARRED POST (exclusive) with one coy. in support at G.36.d.2.5. NOTE:- From this time onwards nothing further has been heard of the three coys. who went forward to occupy its front line.	
"		11.40 am	Message received from 10/11th H.L.I. that our RIGHT flank is in danger.	
"		12.30 pm	Enemy have pressed back the support Coy. and are in line of railway in G.29.c.	
"		1 pm	From this time onwards enemy commenced to press on to Battn. H.Q., and 2nd R.S.F. on its left. Intensity of fire increases gradually.	
"		3 pm	Situation at this time was that the enemy were pressing round our front and flanks. After consultation with O.C. 2nd R.S.F., decision is made to withdraw under mutual fire support and machine gun fire.	
"		3.5 pm	2nd R.S.F. commenced retirement.	
"		3.30 pm	14th H.L.I. commenced retirement.	
"		4 pm	RIVER LYS crossed over bridge at G.21.d.6.2.	

14TH HIGHLAND LIGHT INFANTRY

WAR DIARY 120TH BDE. 40TH DIVISION Army Form C. 2118.

INTELLIGENCE SUMMARY. VOL. XXIII

Page III

APRIL 1918

Place	Date	Hour	Summary of Events and Information	Remarks and references to Appendices
SAILLY SUR LA LYS	9th.	4.30 pm	Battalion occupies trench system about G.21.d.4.7 and holds the bridge head against enemy who are on other bank.	
"		6 pm	Ammunition running short. Conference with Artillery Commander (18 pdrs + 60 pdrs)	
LE PETIT MORTIER		10 pm	Battalion relieved in the trench system by 50TH DIVISION and withdraws to LE PETIT MORTIER.	
"	10th. WED.	3.55 am	Orders received for Units of the 120th Brigade at LE PETIT MORTIER to form a composite Battalion under major SEAGRIM and to move to area at G.27.c & d.	
"		5 am	Battalion marches out of LE PETIT MORTIER.	
A 27 d		6 am	Battn. takes up a position in A.27.d	
"		7.45 am	British (?) aeroplane crosses our lines and signals to us to retire. No notice taken.	
"		8 am	Line of resistance from FROID NID FME inclusive through A.27.d.3.7 to A.26.a.4.1 is dug and manned by the details of the three Battalions.	

14th HIGHLAND LIGHT INFANTRY   120TH BDE.   40TH DIVISION

Army Form C. 2118.

APRIL 1918

WAR DIARY
or
INTELLIGENCE SUMMARY.

VOL. XXIII   PAGE IV

(Erase heading not required.)

Place	Date	Hour	Summary of Events and Information	Remarks and references to Appendices
A 27 d	April 10	11.25 am	Orders received for composite Battalion to man STEENWERCK SWITCH	
		11.45 am	Troops move off. Battn. H.Q. established at A 27 d 5.1. Coy. of YORK'S PIONEERS is left as local reserve at Battn. H.Q.	
		1.50 pm	At 1.50 pm an officer's reconnaissance brought in the following information. The enemy had occupied Q.10 central and had probably crossed the STILBEQUE river at about Q.10 b.d. Troops of the 40th Division held the STEENWERCK SWITCH as far south as Q.10 to 4.8 and 119th Bde. were trying to extend southwards.	
		2.10 pm	The village of KIRLEM is under heavy machine gun fire	
		4.15 pm	Since about 12 NOON the enemy have been pressing against troops holding STEENWERCK SWITCH and these very gradually fell back in front of the road running south through A 24 b + d. Battn. Headquarters moved to A 31 c 1.5.	
		4.35 pm	Few matly reinforcements coming up, so covered instruct troops to hold at all costs.	

14TH HIGHLAND LIGHT INFANTRY. 120TH BDE. 40TH DIVN
APRIL, 1918.

WAR DIARY
or
INTELLIGENCE SUMMARY. VOL. XXIII

Page V

Army Form C. 2118.

Place	Date	Hour	Summary of Events and Information	Remarks and references to Appendices
A 27 d	10th	5.45 pm	Troops on the right of Divisional front falling back everywhere. German M.G. and rifle fire strongly developing. Battn H.Q. with fire and moves to A 20 c 1.7. Composite Battalion of 120th Infy Bde. still held on their roughly in front of road running south through A 24 c+d., and held on to this line all night and until next forenoon. (as indicated below)	
"	"	11.55 pm	Owing to there being a gap between our left flank about A 15 d central, a mixed force of R.E.'s & Gunners was sent out entrenches itself about A 15 central	
THUR 11th.	4:50 am	A party of 200 rifles is sent up to further strengthen the R.E. in A 15 central	
"	11 am	Troops falling back everywhere especially from the direction of LE PETIT MORTIER. Situation on the right critical. Battalion H.Q. moves towards LE VERRIER. and occupies old Brigade H.Q. 700 yds W. of the Cross Roads west of LE VERRIER	

14TH H.L.I. 120th Brigade 40TH DIVISION.
APRIL 1918   Army Form C. 2118.

WAR DIARY
INTELLIGENCE SUMMARY.
VOL. XXIII
Page VI

Place	Date	Hour	Summary of Events and Information	Remarks and references to Appendices
LE VERRIER	11th	12 noon	Situation is as follows which remains practically unchanged throughout the day:- Our line runs along narrow gauge railway due east of LE VERRIER to a point about A.20.c.9.1. thence to Ferme au BOIS and thence echeloned back in a SOUTH WESTERLY direction parallel to the VERRIER – DOULIEU road. Enemy throughout the day holding this line we very much improved.	
		3 pm	A Brigade of the 31st Division slips in under cover of our line on a line running approximately N.E & S.W through the cross roads west of LE VERRIER.	
		4 pm	Enemy began to press on line near Ferme du Bois. Our left falls back a little.	
		4.15 pm	Local reserves sent up. Situation restored on left.	
		4.35 pm	Received preliminary instructions we being relieved.	
		7 pm	Counterattack across frontally 93rd Brigade apparently successful as the night is peaceful.	

14th Th. L. I.
120th Bde. 40th DIVISION

APRIL, 1918.

WAR DIARY
INTELLIGENCE SUMMARY.

Army Form C. 2118.

VOL. XXIII

Page VII

Place	Date	Hour	Summary of Events and Information	Remarks and references to Appendices
STRAZEELE	12th	6am	Relief frustrated for tonight before, takes place, and Battalion marches to STRAZEELE, at 10.30 a.m.	
PRADELLES	"	4pm	Battalion moves to PRADELLE	
"	13th	3pm	Battalion leaves PRADELLES, moves to HONDEGHEM where transport joins column, and marches via ST. MARIE CAPPEL and BAVINCHOVE to ZUYTPEENE and billeted there at midnight.	
ZUYTPEENE	14th	8am	Battalion left ZUYTPEENE and marched via ST. SYZER, OUV PERDU, CLAEMARAIS, ST. OMER to TATINGHEM billets.	
TATINGHEM	15th to 19th	—	Battalion resting and refitting, + exercising	
ACQUIN	20th to 29th		Battalion moved to ACQUIN, and carried on training	

14th H.L.I.   40TH DIVISION   Army Form C. 2118.
120TH BDE.

WAR DIARY
or
INTELLIGENCE SUMMARY.   VOL. XXIII

APRIL 1918

(Erase heading not required.)

Place	Date	Hour	Summary of Events and Information	Remarks and references to Appendices
ACQUIN	30		Battalion (plus 2 composite companies 10/11 H.L.I.) move under orders 1 No 2 composite brigade (H.Q. 119th Bde.) from ACQUIN at 7 am and marched via QUELMES, ETREHEM TATINGHEM, ST. OMER to BONNEGNEM (St. MOMELIN area) to billets there. (C.O and 2ts. Young, Hutchison, Nicholson, Mc Laughlin, Martin, Stewart joined Brigade party at BOISDINGHEM and reconnoitred EAST POPERINGHE line). 30/4/18	H. Mackay, major, commanding 14TH L.I.

WAR DIARY
or
INTELLIGENCE SUMMARY.

Army Form C. 2118.

VOL. XXIII

Casualties during APRIL.

Officers

KILLED	WOUNDED	MISSING or unaccounted for
Capt A.B. Burton. M.C.	Lieut E.D. Johnson.	Capt H.N.S. Mummery.
	" J.R. Barclay	" R.D. Blackledge. M.C
	" R.L.H	" H.V.G. Henderson.
	2/Lieut. P. Frew.	" H.N.S Mummery
		Lieut J.C. Picken. M.C.
		" Lt. K. Reid
		" J.S. Robertson
		Lieut C.C. Jennings
		" A.C. Curle
		" J.R. Barclay
		2/Lt J.D. Edwards.
		" W. Henderson.
5	66	396

O.R.

30/4/18

H. Stracey, Major,
comdg. 14th H.L.I.

14th High. L.I. 20th Inf Bde 40th Division 14 H.L.I.

HEADQUARTERS 120TH INFANTRY BRIGADE
120/146
17/6/18

WAR DIARY or INTELLIGENCE SUMMARY
Army Form C. 2118.

MAY 1918 VOL. XXIV

VOL 24

Place	Date	Hour	Summary of Events and Information	Remarks and references to Appendices
NIEURELET	1		Battn. moved under orders of No 2 Composite Bde. from NIEURELET via LEDERZEELE, BALEMBERG, WAEMAERS CAPPEL, HARDIFORT to RWELD arriving at 2 pm	
RWELD	2		Officers reconnoitred the WATOU - ABEELE line. Battn ordered to move back to ST MOMELIN AREA.	
	3		Moved at 12 n. to BONNEGHEM	
	4		Moved to WATTEN arriving at 3 pm	
WATTEN	5		At WATTEN. Presentation of Medal Ribbands by Maj. General Ponsonby 3 pm	
	6		Officers, NCOs. men watching to establishment of Battn training staff. Left at 1 pm for ST OMER.	
	10		Battn. training staff moved to ESQUELBECQ via MILLAM, BOLLEZEELE, ZEGGERS CAPPEL, arriving in billets at 5 pm	
ESQUELBECQ	12		Brigade Conference at 6 pm. Orders received to reconnoitre the BRIEL sector of the WINNEZEELE LINE.	
	13/31		Daily Reconnaissance of the LINE were made by Officers & NCOs with a view to its establishment on a line of resistance. Daily reports with extract for Bn H.Q., transport lines, roads to be maintained outpost scheme, further of holding the line &c, were submitted to Bde H.Z.	
	31		Presentation of Medal Ribbands by Brig. Genl. Kirkirk D.S.O. 31/5/18	

24 IV label
Yashmaker major
comd 14 H.L.I.

WAR DIARY or INTELLIGENCE SUMMARY

Army Form C. 2118

14th High. L.I. 116th Inf. Bde. – 39th Division

June 1918

Place	Date	Hour	Summary of Events and Information	Remarks and references to Appendices
ESQUELBECQ	1/2		Reconnaissance of WINNIZEELE LINE	
	3		Battn. moved under orders of 120th Inf. Bde. from ESQUELBECQ & RINXENT to LA CAPELLE. Moved by rail to RINXENT - MARQUISE. Train by march to LA CAPELLE, arrived at 11-30 p.m. Attached to 103rd Infy. Bde.	
LA CAPELLE	9/10		Advance Guard of 3/25th American Infantry Regt. to be trained by Battn. Training Staff.	
	11		Battn. march under orders of 103rd Inf. Bde. to SURQUES via BOULOGNE - STONE ROAD	
SURQUES	12/13		Battn. handed out, opened Regimental School for 311th American	
	14		Infantry - Coys. attd; B.H.Q. Boursay; Thursday; Caucheries; H.Q. moved to BRUNEMBERT and took over duties from 19/1st High. L.I.	
	15		and commenced training of 311th Infy. Regt. D Coy 14th High L.I. attached to 1st Bn. 311th Infy Regt. at BRUNEMBERT and HAUTE CREUSE. B Coy attached to 2nd Bn. 311th Infy Regt. at ESCOEUILLES and C Coy attached to 3rd Bn. at VERVAL.	
BRUNEMBERT	16/30		Training of 311th Infy. Regt. continued. Battalion transferred to 116th Infy Bde on 17th June.	

30/6/18

Hysmackay Lt. Col.
Comdg. 14 th H.L.I.

14th High. L.I.

WAR DIARY
of
INTELLIGENCE SUMMARY.

Army Form C. 2118.

July 1918

Place	Date	Hour	Summary of Events and Information	Remarks and references to Appendices
BRUNEMBERT	1/19		Battalion Training. Staff continued training 311th American Infantry Regiment.	
FOUFFLIN-RECAMETZ	20/31	6	Lt.-Col. J.F.N. BAXENDALE returned to duty and took over command from Major (A/Lt-Col) H.G.S. MACKAY.	
BRUNEMBERT		19	Battn. moved under orders of 116th Infy Bde with 311th American Infantry Regiment to FOUFFLIN-RECAMETZ by march route to LOTTINGHEM where it entrained for LIGNY ST FLOCHEL. Battn H.Q. attached to Regimental H.Q. 311th American Infantry Regiment located at FOUFFLIN-RECAMETZ. D Coy attached 1st Battn at ST MICHEL - B Coy attached 2nd Battn at MESNIL ST POL and C Coy attached 3rd Bn at TERVAS	

J.F.N. Baxendale Lt-col
Commanding 14th Highl. L.I.

31/7/18

66TH DIVISION
TRAINING CADRES

40 DIV
120 Bde

14TH BN H. L. I.
AUG - DEC 1918

1918 AUG to 1919 APR

~~From~~ 40 DIV
120 Bde

Served with 197 Bde
L of C. from Sept 1918

14th Highland Light Infantry

27 N
3 sheets

66/44 34
42/720

Army Form C. 2118.

WAR DIARY
or
INTELLIGENCE SUMMARY.

(Erase heading not required.)

August 1918.

Vol 27 Page I

Instructions regarding War Diaries and Intelligence Summaries are contained in F. S. Regs., Part II. and the Staff Manual respectively. Title pages will be prepared in manuscript.

Place	Date	Hour	Summary of Events and Information	Remarks and references to Appendices
FOUQUIÈRES-RICAMERZ (Ref. LENS II)	1		Battalion training. Staff continued training of 3115 American Infantry Regt.	
	2			
	3			
	4		In accordance with 116th Infy Bde Order No 250 Battalion moved to TINCQUES and entrained for LIGQUES and AUDRUICQ and marched to LOUCHES	
	5		Battalion detrained at AUDRUICQ and marched to LOUCHES and billeted there.	
LOUCHES (Ref HAZEBROUCK 5A)	6			
"	7			
"	8			
"	9			
"	10			
"	11			
"	12			
"	13			
"	14			
"	15		In accordance with 39th Divisional Order No 241 the Battalion marched to NORTKERQUE and entrained. Battalion detrained at ABANCOURT and marched to camp. Battalion came under orders of G.O.C. 66th Division.	
ABANCOURT (Ref DIEPPE)	16			
	17			
	18			
	19			

J M Bore??? Lt Col
14 HLI

14th Highland Light Infantry

WAR DIARY
~~INTELLIGENCE SUMMARY~~

Army Form C. 2118.

August 1918.

Page 2

Place	Date	Hour	Summary of Events and Information	Remarks and references to Appendices
ABANCOURT	20			
"	21			
"	22			
HAUDRICOURT (Ref. 16.)	23		In accordance with Centre Camp Orders No. 3 Battalion moves to New Camp near HAUDRICOURT.	
	24		Battalion came under orders of C.R.E. 66th Division, Cant Commanding QUESNES Camp.	
			Capt. H.G.S. MACKAY transferred to 1/5th Bn. Seaforth Highlanders (Army) A.G's No. 2158/4505 (0) d/11/8/18 C.R. No.1364/4950 C.)	
	25			
	26			
	27			
	28			
	29		Battalion came under orders of G.O.C. 199th Infantry Bde.	
	30			
	31			

J.H. Bassewade Hill
Lt. Col.
14th Bn.

CONFIDENTIAL.

WAR DIARY

OF

14th. HIGHLAND LIGHT INFANTRY.

From 1st. September 1918.   To 30th. September 1918.

(VOLUME FOUR.)

14th Highland Light Infantry.

WAR DIARY
~~INTELLIGENCE SUMMARY.~~

September 1918

Army Form C. 2118.

Page 1

Place	Date	Hour	Summary of Events and Information	Remarks and references to Appendices
HAVRINCOURT (Ref. 1b) DIEPPE	1	00:09.		
	2	00:09.		
	3	00:09.		
	4	00:09.		
	5	00:09.		
	6	00:09.		
	7	00:09.		
	8	00:09.		
	9	00:09.		
	10	00:09.		
	11	00:09.		
	12	00:09.		
	13	00:09.		
	14	00:09.		
	15	00:09.		
	16	00:09.	Captain S.M. MACKENZIE R.A.M.C. J.C. 2/Lieut D.R. CAMPBELL knickling 1/Lieut F.G. CADIZ knickling knickleus reported for duty. knickt.	
	17	00:09.	1 Sergeant and 4 privates from the Cameron Highlanders and 4 privates from The Royal Scots reported. 00:09.	
	18			

J.G.Rahn Captain
Commanding 14 H.L.I.

14 Highland Light Infantry

WAR DIARY
or
INTELLIGENCE SUMMARY

(Erase heading not required.)

Army Form C. 2118.

September 1918

Page 2.

Place	Date	Hour	Summary of Events and Information	Remarks and references to Appendices
HAUDRICOURT	19			
(Rd) DIEPPE	20			
(6)	21			
	22.		53 other ranks from The Black Watch reported. W54.	
	23.		W54.	
	24.		54 other ranks from The Border Regiment reported. W54.	
	25.		3 other ranks from the Scottish Rifles and 2 other ranks from the Royal Scottish Fusiliers reported. W54.	
	26.		W54.	
	27		11 other ranks from the Cameron Highlanders, 121 other ranks from Lovats Scouts, 6 other ranks from The Scottish Horse, 31 other ranks from the Black Watch, 22 other ranks from the Argyll & Sutherland Highlanders, 4 other ranks from the Royal Scots and 3 other ranks from The Border Regiment reported. W54.	
	28		Lt. P.H. MARSHALL, the Black Watch, and 73 other ranks from The Black Watch reported. W54.	
	29.		W54.	
	30		W54.	

Y.P. Palm Captain
Commanding 14 H.L.I.

CONFIDENTIAL.

WAR DIARY.

OF

14th. HIGHLAND LIGHT INFANTRY.

From 1st. OCTOBER, 1918.

TO 31st. OCTOBER, 1918.

(VOLUME FIVE)

CONFIDENTIAL.

D.A.G.,
G.H.Q.,
3rd. Echelon,
BASE.

October, 1918.

Herewith copy of War Diary for the month of

[signature] Lt. Col.

Commanding 14th. H.L. Infantry.

1.11.18.

14th Highland Light Infantry. Page 1.

Army Form C. 2118.

WAR DIARY
or
INTELLIGENCE SUMMARY.
(Erase heading not required.)

October 1918

Instructions regarding War Diaries and Intelligence Summaries are contained in F. S. Regs., Part II. and the Staff Manual respectively. Title pages will be prepared in manuscript.

Place	Date	Hour	Summary of Events and Information	Remarks and references to Appendices
HAUDRICOURT (Ref DIEPPE 16)	1.		Training of Malarial Reinforcements work on camp. W.D.9.	
	2.		Do Do W.D.9.	
	3.		Do Do W.D.9.	
	4.		Do Do W.D.9.	
			2nd Lieut. F.G. CADIZ and 2nd Lieut. D.R. CAMPBELL proceeded to join the 5th Royal Inniskilling Fusiliers to which they have been posted.	
			The undernoted reinforcements reported :-	
			26 other ranks from the Black Watch	
			126 other ranks from the Argyll & Sutherland Highlanders.	
			4 other ranks from the Royal Scots	
			24 other ranks from the Scottish Rifles.	
			8 other ranks from the (S.H.) Black Watch.	
			2 other ranks from the Border Regiment. W.D.9.	
	5.		4 other ranks from The Black Watch (S.H.) proceeded to join 51st Division. W.D.9.	
			The following Reinforcement reported.	
			One private from the Argyll & Sutherland Highlanders, who had been detained for 24 hours on account of sickness.	
			Training of Malarial Reinforcements and work on camp. W.D.9.	
	6.		Church Parade W.D.9.	
	7.		Training of Malarial Reinforcements and work on camp W.D.9.	
	8.		Do W.D.9.	
			The following reinforcement reported, one private from the Black Watch reporting from Hospital W.D.9.	

29 N
Ashes

terminated 14 H.L.I.

14 Highland Light Infantry Page 2.

Army Form C. 2118.

WAR DIARY
INTELLIGENCE SUMMARY

October 1918

Place	Date	Hour	Summary of Events and Information	Remarks and references to Appendices
HAUDRICOURT (Ref: DIEPPE)(b)	9		120 other ranks of the Cameron Highlanders (boat scouts) proceeded to join the 10th Battalion Cameron Highlanders. Authority 197th Infantry Brigade 2083/3/a WO9.	
	10		Training of Malarial reinforcements and work on camp. WO9.	
	11		The undernoted reinforcements reported:—	
			13 other ranks from the Argyll and Sutherland Highlanders	
			40 other ranks from the Cameron Highlanders (boat scouts)	
			1 other rank from the Border Regiment.	
			Training of Malarial reinforcements and work on camp. WO9.	
	12		40 other ranks of the Cameron Highlanders (boat scouts) proceeded to join the 10th Battalion Cameron Highlanders. Authority 197th Infantry Brigade 2083/3/A WO9.	
			Training of Malarial reinforcements and work on camp. WO9.	
			12 other ranks from the B'lack Watch reported. WO9.	
			Church Parade.	
	13		Training of Malarial Reinforcements & work on camp. WO9.	
	14		Do	
	15		Three other ranks from the Black Watch reported	
	16		Training of Malarial Reinforcements and work on camp WO9.	
	17		1 other rank from the Black Watch reported	
			Training of Malarial Reinforcements and work on camp WO9.	

J.W. Lawrence Lt Col
Commanding 14 H.L.I

Army Form C. 2118.

14th Highland Light Infantry

WAR DIARY
or
INTELLIGENCE SUMMARY. October 1918

Page 3.

Place	Date	Hour	Summary of Events and Information	Remarks and references to Appendices
HAUDRICOURT (Rly DIEPPE)	18/10/18		1 other rank from The Royal Scots reported. Training of Malarial Reinforcements work on camp W2Y.	
	19.		Do Do	
	20.		The undermentioned reinforcements reported :— 10 other ranks from The Cameron Highlanders. 6 " " The Lovat Scouts Cameron Highlanders (Lovat Scouts) 3 " " The Black Watch 1 " " The Scottish Horse Black Watch (Scottish Horse) 10 " " The Royal Scots 6 " " The Borderers 1 " " The Scottish Rifles.	
	21.		Church Parade W2Y. Training of Malarial Reinforcements work on camp. 4 other ranks from The Cameron Highlanders (Lovat Scouts) proceeded to join the 10th Battalion Cameron Highlanders. W2Y.	
	22.		The following reinforcements reported, 20 other ranks from The Black Watch. Training of Malarial Reinforcements work on camp. W2Y.	
	23.		Training of Malarial Reinforcements work on camp W2Y.	

J.P.H. Tennant Lt Col
Commanding 14th H.L.I.

14th Highland Light Infantry.

Page 4.

Army Form C. 2118.

WAR DIARY
or
INTELLIGENCE SUMMARY.   October 1918
(Erase heading not required.)

Place	Date	Hour	Summary of Events and Information	Remarks and references to Appendices
HAUDRI COURT (Ref. DIEPPE) (6)	24		The following other ranks proceeded to join the battalions mentioned – Authority 197th Infantry Brigade 2263/1/A.	
			22 other ranks from the Border Regt. proceeded to join the 2nd Munster Regt.	
			93 " " The Black Watch " " " 13th Black Watch	
			5 " " The Cameron Highlanders " " " 1st Cameron.	
			8.5 " " The Argyll & Sutherland Highlanders " " " 10th A. & S. H.	
			4 " " The Royal Scots " " " 2nd Royal Scots	
			10 " " The Scottish Rifles " " " 1st Scottish Rifles	
	25.		Training of Material reinforcements & work on camp.	W.t.O.9.
	26.		Do	W.t.O.9.
	27.		Do	W.t.O.9. X The other ranks from the Black Watch who had reported at AUMALE were returned today.
	28.		Church Parade. One other rank from the Black Watch (Scottish Horse) reported.	X W.t.O.9. to W.t.O.9.
	29.		Training of Material reinforcements & work on camp.	W.t.O.9.
	30.		Do. One Sergeant-Instructor reported for duty.	W.t.O.9.
	31.		Training of Material reinforcements & work on camp. Do.	W.t.O.9.

J.K.W. Barendon Lt. Col.
Commanding 14 H.L.I.

C O N F I D E N T I A L.

WAR DIARY.

OF

14th. HIGHLAND LIGHT INFANTRY.

From 1st. November, 1918.

To 30th. November, 1918.

VOLUME Five.

114 Highland Light Infantry

WAR DIARY
INTELLIGENCE SUMMARY.

November 1918 Page 1

Army Form C. 2118.

Place	Date	Hour	Summary of Events and Information	Remarks and references to Appendices
HAUDRI: COURT (by DIEPPE 16)	1/11/18		Training of Malarial Reinforcements and work on camp. W.E.F.	
	2/11/18		Do. Do.	
			The following reinforcements reported:	
			5 other ranks from the Black Watch	
			8 " " " the Black Watch (Scottish Horse)	
			14 " " " the Argyll & Sutherland Highlanders	
			14 " " " the Cameron Highlanders (Lovat Scouts)	
			" " " the Border Regiment. W.E.F.	
	3/11/18		Church Parade.	
			The following reinforcements reported:	
			2 other ranks from the Argyll & Sutherland Highlanders	
			& other rank from the Black Watch (Scottish Horse)	
			The following reinforcements proceeded to join the 10th (R.S.) Cameron Highlanders in accordance with 197th Infantry Brigade 3260/A.Q. of 2/11/18 W.E.F.	
			17 other ranks from the Cameron Highlanders (Lovat Scouts) W.E.F.	
	4/11/18		Training of Malarial reinforcements and work on camp.	
			The following reinforcements reported	
			40 other ranks from the Black Watch (Scottish Horse) W.E.F.	
	5/11/18		Training of Malarial Reinforcements & work on camp.	
			Lieut. P.H. MARSHALL The Black Watch (Scottish Horse) reported for duty.	
			One other rank from The Black Watch (Scottish Horse) reported. W.E.F.	

14 Highland Light Infantry   November 1918

WAR DIARY
INTELLIGENCE SUMMARY.
Page 2.

Army Form C. 2118.

Place	Date	Hour	Summary of Events and Information	Remarks and references to Appendices
HAUDRI- COURT DIEPPE (Ref.16)	6/11/18		Training of Malarial Reinforcements ranks on camp. Reinforcements proceeded to join the undernoted battalions in accordance with 197th Infantry Brigade 2262/2/A.Q. of 5/11/18 :— 3 other ranks from the Cameron Highlanders to the 5th Cameron Highlanders. 8 " " " " " The Royal Scots to the 17th Royal Scots. wef sty	
	7/11/18		Training of Malarial Reinforcements rank on camp. Reinforcements proceeded to join the undernoted battalions in accordance with 197th Infantry Brigade 2265/2/A.Q. of 5/11/18 :— 21 other ranks from the Argyll & Sutherland Highlanders to the 2nd Argyll & Sutherland Highlanders. wef sty 5 " " " The Seaforth Rifles to the 1st Scottish Rifles.	
	8/11/18		Training of Malarial Reinforcements work on camp. Reinforcements proceeded to join the undernoted battalions in accordance with 197th Infantry Brigade 2262/2/A.Q. of 5/11/18 :— 13 other ranks from the Black Watch to the 13th Black Watch. wef sty 4 " " " " " The Black Watch (SH) to do 16 " " " " The Borders " " " the 6th Lancashire Fusiliers. wef sty	
	9/11/18		Training of Malarial Reinforcements rank on camp. Church Parades.	
	10/11/18		One other rank from the Lancashire Fusiliers (formerly Border Regt) reported LRC69. wef sty	
	11/11/18		Training of Malarial Reinforcements Work on camp.	

MCGillan Lt.
A/Adjt. 14 H.L.I.

14 Highland Light Infantry

WAR DIARY
or
INTELLIGENCE SUMMARY.
(Erase heading not required.)

Army Form C. 2118.

November 1918
Page 3.

Place	Date	Hour	Summary of Events and Information	Remarks and references to Appendices
HAUDRI: COURT. (Reference - DIEPPE)	12/11/18		Training of Material Reinforcements work in camp. W19.	
	13/11/18		Do Do	
	14/11/18		2nd Lieut. J. JONES Argyll Sutherland Highlanders reported for duty. One other rank from The Black Watch (Scottish Horse) reported. W19.	
	15/11/18		Training of Material reinforcements work in camp. W19. Do Do	
			One other rank from The Black Watch reported. W19.	
	16/11/18		Training of Material reinforcements work in camp. W19.	
	17/11/18		Do W19.	
	18/11/18		Do W19.	
	19/11/18		Do W19.	
	20/11/18		Do W19.	
	21/11/18		Do W19.	
	22/11/18		Do W19.	
	23/11/18		Do W19.	
			One other rank from The Black Watch (Scottish Horse) reported W19.	
	24/11/18		Church Parade. One other rank from The Black Watch reported. The/	W. W. Gillan Lt. a/Adjt 14 H.L.I.

14 Highland Light Infantry

November 1918

Army Form C. 2118.

Page 4.

WAR DIARY
or
INTELLIGENCE SUMMARY.
(Erase heading not required.)

Place	Date	Hour	Summary of Events and Information	Remarks and references to Appendices
HAI. DRI. COURT. (Reserve) DIEPPE (b)	21/11/18		The following reinforcements proceeded to join the undermentioned battalions in accordance with 197th Infantry Brigade 3372/A of 22/11/18:-	
			(CH) 9 Other ranks from the Cameron Highlanders to the 5th Cameron Highlanders.	
			9 " " " " " 4/5 Black Watch.	
			4 " " " " " the Royal Scots " 5/6 Royal Scots.	
			16 " " " " " the Argyll & Sutherland Highlanders to the 1/6 Argyll & Sutherland Highlanders.	
			Training of Material Reinforcements & work on camp.	
	25/11/18		The following reinforcements proceeded to join the undermentioned battalions in accordance with 197th Infantry Brigade 3372/3/A of 23/11/18:-	
			2 other ranks from the Cameron Highlanders to the 1st Cameron Highlanders.	
			2 " " " " " Black Watch " 1st Black Watch.	
			9 " " " " " The Black Watch (Scottish Horse) " 13th (S.H.) Black Watch.	
			2 " " " " " the Border Regiment " 7th Border Regiment.	
			5 " " " " " the Border Regiment " 5th Connaught Rangers.	
			1 " " " " " the Scottish Rifles " 1st Scottish Rifles.	
	26/11/18 27/11/18 28/11/18 29/11/18 30/11/18		Training of Material Reinforcements and work on camp.	

J. M. M. Reynolds A.Col.
Commanding 14 H.L.I.

14th Highland Light Infantry   December 1918   Army Form C. 2118.

WAR DIARY
INTELLIGENCE SUMMARY.
(Erase heading not required.)

Instructions regarding War Diaries and Intelligence Summaries are contained in F. S. Regs., Part II. and the Staff Manual respectively. Title pages will be prepared in manuscript.

Vol 31   Page 1.

Place	Date	Hour	Summary of Events and Information	Remarks and references to Appendices
HAUDRI- COURT (Rly: DIEPPE)	1/12/18		Church Parade. W.9.	
	2/12/18		Training of Malarial reinforcements rwork on camp. W.9.	
	3/12/18		In accordance with 197th Infantry Brigade Order S/27 dated 2/12/18 the following other ranks were handed over to the 16th Battalion Sherwood Foresters:—	
			81 other ranks of the Black Watch	
			58 " " Black Watch (Scottish Horse)	
			84 " " Argyll & Sutherland Highlanders	
			10 " " Cameron Highlanders	
			12 " " Scottish Rifles	
			2 " " Royal Scots Fusiliers	
			30 " " Border Regiment	
			12 " " Royal Scots	
			1 " " Lancashire Fusiliers	
			In accordance with 197th Infantry Brigade Order S/27/1 dated 2/12/18 the following re-postings took place :—	
			Lieut. P.H. MARSHALL 13th Black Watch attached 14.H.L.I. to 16th Sherwood Foresters	
			2/Lieut. J. JONES Argyll & Sutherland Highlanders " " D°.	
4/12/18			W.9.	
5/12/18			W.9.	
6/12/18			W.9.	
7/12/18			W.9.	

14th Highland Light Infantry December 1918 Army Form C. 2118.

WAR DIARY
or
INTELLIGENCE SUMMARY.
(Erase heading not required.)   Page 2.

Place	Date	Hour	Summary of Events and Information	Remarks and references to Appendices
HAUDRI-COURT. (Ry:DIEPPE)	8/12/18			
	9/12/18		10.08A	
	10/12/18		10.08A	
			In accordance with 197th Infantry Brigade Order S.30 dated 9.12.18 the battalion entrained at AUMALE station and proceeded to HAVRE	
HAVRE	11/12/18		10.08A	
	12/12/18		10.09A	
	13/12/18		10.09A	
	14/12/18		10.08A	
	15/12/18		10.08A	
	16/12/18		10.08A	
	17/12/18		10.09A	
	18/12/18		10.09A	
	19/12/18		Sun.B	
	20/12/18		Sun.B	
	21/12/18		Sun.B	
	22/12/18		Sun.B	
	23/12/18		In accordance with 116th Infantry Brigade Order N°5° dated 21/12/18 1st Battalion was transferred to N°1 REST CAMP A section LE HAVRE In accordance with 194th Infantry Bde. letter 3903/8 dated 21/12/18 2nd LT J JONES A & H returned and was attached for duty	

14th Highland Light Infantry November 1918

WAR DIARY
INTELLIGENCE SUMMARY
Army Form C. 2118.
Page 3

Place	Date	Hour	Summary of Events and Information	Remarks and references to Appendices
HAVRE	24/12/18		The Battalion took over No 1 Rest Camp "A" Section for the purpose of receiving men proceeding to Chiseldon and Duddingston for Demobilization	
	25/12/18		Christmas Day	
	26/12/18		46 O.R. reported proceeding to CHISELDON (36) DUDDINGSTON (10)	
	27/12/18		43 O.R. reported proceeding to CHISELDON (29) DUDDINGSTON (14)	
	28/12/18		839 O.R. reported proceeding to CHISELDON and DUDDINGSTON. 97 O.R. proceeded to "B" Section No 1 Camp en route for CHISELDON and DUDDINGSTON	
	29/12/18		Receiving and despatching O.R. for DUDDINGSTON only. Arrivals 1027. Despatches 305.	
	30/12/18		Arrivals 241. Despatches 305.	
	31/12/18		Arrivals 34. Despatches 341.	

TRAINING CADRE
~~39TH DIVISION~~
~~DIVL TROOPS~~

197 BDE

66 DIVISION

14TH BN HIGH'D LT INFY
JAN - APR 1919

3025

FROM 40 DIV RoBk

1 7 H 41

January 1919
116th Brigade 39th Division
14th Highland L.I.

War Diary and Intelligence Summary

Summary of Events and Information

Date 1919			
Jan 1st	Arrivals 605 Offrs and other ranks. To Dispersal Camp 605 Offrs & O.R.		
2	" " 123 " " " " 123 " "		
3	" " 913 " " " " 913 " "		
4	" " 331 " " " " 331 " "		
5	" " 209 " " " " 209 " "		
6	" " 109 " " " " 109 " "		
7	" " 50 " " " " 50 " "		
8	Captain P.A. Marshall Scottish Horse joined for attachment		
9	Arrivals 618 Offrs & O.R. To Dispersal bands 618 Offrs & O.R.		
10	" " 318 " " " " "		
11	" " 445 " " " " "		
12	" " 441 " " " " "		
13	" " 583 " " " " "		
14	" " 360 " " " " "		
15	" " 1536 " " " " "		

January 1919. 116th Brigade. 39th Division
War Diary and Intelligence Summary. 1st Highland L.I.

Date 1919	Summary of Events and Information	
Jan 17	Arrivals 139 Offrs & OR departures for disturbed area 139 Offrs & OR. Left B[atalio]n for demobilization 402 Offrs & OR	
18	" " " " " " 402 " " "	
19	" " " " " " " " "	
20	" " " " " " " " "	
21	Arrivals 817 Offrs & OR. departure for disturbed areas 817. Offrs & OR	
22	835 " " " " " 835 " "	
23	372 " " " " " 372 " "	
24	464 " " " " " 464 " "	
25	Departure of Patrol left B[atalio]n for demobilization	
26	—	
27	Arrivals 409 Offrs & OR departure for disturbed area 409 Offrs & OR	
28	308 " " " " " 308 " "	
29	698 " " " " " 698 " "	
30	Handed over duties at W Camp to 2nd Middlesex R[e]g[imen]t and moved to Offa Tering Camp S[e]rvice for duty	
31		

A. Murray Cap[tai]n
for Lt Col
1/4 H.L.I.

SECRET.

Army Form C. 2118.

14TH BATTALION, HIGHLAND LIGHT INFANTRY.

WAR DIARY or INTELLIGENCE SUMMARY.

(Erase heading not required.)

Instructions regarding War Diaries and Intelligence Summaries are contained in F. S. Regs, Part II. and the Staff Manual respectively. Title pages will be prepared in manuscript.

Place	Date	Hour	Summary of Events and Information	Remarks and references to Appendices
Le Havre	July 1		Battalion employed as machinery of demobilization at No. 1 Dispatching Camp	
"	2		ditto	
"	3		ditto	
"	4		ditto	
"	5		ditto	
"	6		ditto	
"	7		ditto	
"	8		ditto	
"	9		ditto	
"	10		ditto	
"	11		ditto	
"	12		ditto	
"	13		ditto	
"	14		ditto	
"	15		ditto	
"	16		ditto	
"	17		ditto	
"	18		ditto	
"	19		ditto	
"	20		ditto	
"	21		ditto	
"	22		ditto	
"	23		ditto	
"	24		ditto	
"	25		ditto	
"	26		ditto	
"	27		ditto	
"	28		ditto	

WAR DIARY
or
INTELLIGENCE SUMMARY.

(Erase heading not required.)

Army Form C. 2118.

SECRET

Instructions regarding War Diaries and Intelligence Summaries are contained in F. S. Regs. Part II. and the Staff Manual respectively. Title pages will be prepared in manuscript.

Place	Date	Hour	Summary of Events and Information	Remarks and references to Appendices
Le Havre	March 1		Battalion Cadre employed as Machinery of Demobilization at No 1 Dispatching Camp.	
	2		do	
	3		do	
	4		do	
	5		do	
	6		do	
	7		do	
	8		do	
	9		do	
	10		do	
	11		do	
	12		do	
	13		do	
	14		do	
	15		do	
	16		do	
	17		do	
	18		do	
	19		do	
	20		do	
	21		do	
	22		do	
	23		do	
	24		do	
	25		do	
	26		do	
	27		do	
	28		do	
	29		do	
	30		do	
	31		do	

R. Mucalpan. Lt.Col.
7/11th H.L.I. (T.F.) O.C.

14th Highland Light Infantry
April 1919

WAR DIARY
or
INTELLIGENCE SUMMARY

Army Form C. 2118.

Place	Date 1919	Hour	Summary of Events and Information	Remarks and references to Appendices
SANVIC LE HAVRE	April 1 2 3 4 5 6 7 8 9 10 11 12 13 14 15 16 17 18 19 20 21 22 23 24 25 26 27 28 29 30		Employed on machinery of demobilization personnel at No 1 Debarkating Camp.	

Murisson Captain
Highland L.I.

www.ingramcontent.com/pod-product-compliance
Lightning Source LLC
Chambersburg PA
CBHW081540160426
43191CB00011B/1801